S·15

developing values
with
exceptional children

developing values with exceptional children

SIDNEY B. SIMON

Professor of Humanistic Education
University of Massachusetts

ROBERT D. O'ROURKE

Psychologist
Ft. Collins, Colorado Schools

PRENTICE-HALL, INC. ENGLEWOOD CLIFFS, NEW JERSEY 07632

Library of Congress Cataloging in Publication Data

Simon, Sidney B. (date).
  Developing values with exceptional children.

   Includes bibliographical references.
   1.–Exceptional children.–2.–Values.–3.–Humanistic
psychology.–I.—O'Rourke, Robert D. (date) joint
author.–II.–Title.
BF723.E9S57   370.15′4   76-39786
ISBN 0-13-205310-1

PRENTICE-HALL INTERNATIONAL, INC., *London*
PRENTICE-HALL OF AUSTRALIA PTY. LIMITED, *Sydney*
PRENTICE-HALL OF CANADA, LTD., *Toronto*
PRENTICE-HALL OF INDIA PRIVATE LIMITED, *New Delhi*
PRENTICE-HALL OF JAPAN, INC., *Tokyo*
PRENTICE-HALL OF SOUTHEAST ASIA PTE. LTD., *Singapore*
WHITEHALL BOOKS LIMITED, *Wellington, New Zealand*

To all those teachers who struggle and care enough
to reach children other teachers can't touch

contents

preface

It has been ten years since Kimball Wiles wrote these lines about Louis Raths, his teacher, and the man behind the theory and process of values clarification, " . . . Raths intrigued me with his reactions to my comments. As far as I could detect he never really approved any statement I made. He would ask a question, make a noncommital observation, test my assertion by supplying additional data, ask if I had considered a different alternative . . . I received more questions and the expectation that I would continue to probe."[1]

Louis Raths believed that values were arrived at through a process of choosing freely, choosing from alternatives, choosing after thoughtful consideration of the consequences of each alternative, prizing and cherishing the value, giving it affirmation, acting upon the choice and repeating the value as a pattern of life.[2]

We ask teachers, as they adapt our techniques, to use the "valuing process" or, as Raths wrote, "The idea is, without moralizing, to raise a

---

[1]Wiles, Kimball in the "Foreword" to *Values And Teaching*, by Louis E. Raths, Merrill Harmin, Sidney Simon, Chas. E. Merrill, Columbus, Ohio, 1966, pg. VII
[2]Ibid, pp 28-29

few questions, leave them hanging in the air, and then move on." [3] With this gentle questioning approach you too will be able to help students ponder the deeper meanings of a life philosophy that embraces well-thought-out personal values.

In this small book we have drawn heavily from those men who have most influenced our own lives and work—all of them warm human beings: The late Abraham Maslow and Sidney Jourard, Carl Rogers, Nick Hobbs, Victor Frankl, and Louis Raths. There were so many writers, composers, singers who got under our skins too—Leo Buscaglia, Sam Keen, John Steinbeck, the team of Rodgers and Hammerstein, Tom T. Hall, and John Denver—to name just a few. We will always be indebted to all of these people, who have added meaning to our own development and have had such an impact upon our view of humankind.

---

[3] Ibid, pg. 55

developing values
with
exceptional children

ONE

introduction

THE AUTHORS

This introduction explains how Sid Simon, nationally acclaimed lecturer on Values Clarification and university professor for Humanistic Study from Leverett, Massachusetts and I, Bob O'Rourke, school psychologist and Director of Guidance from Fort Collins, Colorado, got together to write a book. Sid was conducting a weekend Values Clarification Workshop in Denver, Colorado, and I was among the 250 principals, teachers, nurses, counselors, social workers, and ministers who came to clarify their own personal values as well as to acquire strategies for helping those they worked with "back home."

Sid began the first session by asking all of us to write our first names in the center of a sheet of paper, a strategy he calls, "The Name Tag Strategy." Along the right side of the paper he asked for a list:

> Two things you do well with your hands.
> What you are looking forward to next month.
> Two things you want to do before you die.
> One or two things that restored your faith in people this past week.
> Two people who nourish you.
> A place where you have experienced a deep, intense love.

Along the left side of the sheet he requested another inventory:

> Your favorite piece of music.
> Where you would rather be than here.
> Where you remember spending five delicious days in a row.
> Two people with whom you have unfinished business.
> What has been important enough for you to cry about this past year.
> Two things you like about yourself.

We then held out our name tags so that others could read them and we moved, nonverbally, disclosing those events we had written about and reading similar incidents from others lives—an initial way to become involved, to know others and be known by them.

Each response I had written was "clarifying"—but one in particular intrigued me. In reply to the statement: "Write one or two things you would like to do before you die," I had set down, "I would like to write one or two good books before I die." Zing! Where did *that* come from.

2

That obviously came from inside me. Curious. Intriguing. I would think more about this surprising idea in the days to come.

In the short, two-day workshop we were exposed to dozens of values clarification strategies. We learned a process that was practically applicable to life: Choosing, prizing, acting, feeling, validating. Afterwards, as I drove home along the highway bordering the foothills of the Rocky Mountains, I felt validated, which is feeling real good about oneself.

Three months later, vacation over, I was back working with difficult, troubled elementary age children. I was adapting Sid's concepts as well as developing new values clarification strategies of my own. After each session with the children I went back to my office and hastily scribbled notes to myself as to how the strategy might be improved and made more useful next time. Then I thought, "I bet Sid would be interested in what is happening out here." On this impulse I phoned him and explained that I was using humanistic strategies and values clarification with emotionally disturbed and learning disabled kids (that label again). I asked if he would be interested in sharing ideas and writing a book together. (In this world you sometimes have to ask for what you want, realizing that there are those who are willing to help you—another of Sid's discoveries).

Sid thought the book a fascinating idea. In the next few minutes sparks of ideas were brainstormed. We shared ideas, scribbled notes, met occasionally, talked on the phone, read, compared, taped, and annotated. Slowly, fitfully there emerged this book of new strategies especially designed and field tested with "difficult" elementary age children but equally as useful with normal children. We hope our ideas will become useful tools in helping develop the latent potential of those whose lives you touch.

THE SCHOOL

Boxelder is a small rural school located east of Fort Collins, Colorado on Highway 14. The school was built in 1919 and is now a part of the Poudre R-1 School District. "Poudre" is the French name for powder (in this case gun powder) and has significance for the area. In November, 1836, a band of French trappers en route from St. Louis, Missouri to Green River, Wyoming were caught in a blinding snow storm that lasted several days. They were camped beside a river that cascaded down from the mountains. When the weather cleared the order was given to "lighten the wagons" because of the deep snow. The men "cached" (dug a deep pit) beside the river and stored hundreds of pounds of powder, thus concealing the supplies from the Arapahoe Indians who hunted in the area. The Cache La Poudre River, named after this incident, flows out of the mountains near Boxelder School. The Boxelder tree for which the school was named grows abundantly along the river.

The school is staffed with two teachers: Nancy Burgess and Al Kuehnast; Ginney Gillespie and Patrice Bigge are teacher's aides. Donna Wahlen spends a half day a week as visiting nurse; Marlane Diemer, speech therapist, has one full day with the children as does Cassandra Knight, occupational therapist. Judi Yoder gives the equivalent of a half day each week as secretary to the school and Bob O'Rourke is psychologist/director.

On the ground level, the building consists of a kitchen, dining area, an all-purpose room, and restrooms. Upstairs are three classrooms, a crafts area, and a time-out room where children can go to be alone.

The playground is surrounded by trees and bounded by irrigation ditches which, in the summer, carry water to the beet and corn fields. Beyond the farm lands lies the spectacular front range of the Rocky Mountains in panoramic view.

The German people named their early grades of school "kindergarten" meaning a children's garden. We hope the peaceful setting, the ecology, and the people combine to make Boxelder a garden place for children.

THE CHILDREN

We will not spend too much space on writing about the children at Boxelder School. In the following pages you will come to know them quite well. They are labeled with two essential tags when they come to us: "emotionally disturbed" and "learning disabled." For some of you these tags may mean something. We state flatly at the beginning that we don't like labels! We don't like what these word labels usually do! A word is just a few meaningless phonetic symbols side by side. You give it meaning and then it sticks with you. You give it a cognitive meaning, and then you live with it. Dr. Timothy Leary did some fantastic work on the mind when he was at Harvard. He said, "Words are a freezing of validity. . . . Everything that happens is filtered through this stuck, frozen system, and that keeps us from growing."[1] After we receive these "troubled" children, we try desperately to go beyond that frozen concept and see

[1]Buscaglia, Leo, *Love*, Chas. B. Slack, New Jersey, 1972, p. 14.

each of them as individuals, perhaps lonely, angry, and confused, but also capable of loving and caring. We "invite" them as Sidney Jourard said, "to surprise us" and reveal ever new "facets of their being." We become "wonderers," . . . adopt the set that all . . . concepts are tentative and provisional."[2] In one or two years when we "terminate" them and send them back to the regular school we say to teachers, "this is a great kid, you're gonna enjoy having him (or her) in your class," and usually they do. "Great kids" aren't as scary as "emotionally disturbed," "brain damaged," "retarded," "learning disordered" kids. Of course, in the following pages all the children's names have been changed, but they are all human beings between the ages of six and twelve. They are some-times withdrawn, sometimes explosive, and no doubt about it, in the beginning, "difficult," but we hope in our work with them to help them feel, believe and value. Without these human qualities they are destined to long lifetimes of anguish and despair. We give them opportunities to release some of their trapped toxic feelings and in that way make room for more joy and caring. Each time an unhealthy feeling is "let go," energy is made available for more creative purposes.

Helping children discharge or release their toxic feelings is most often achieved through acts of sublimation: yelling, pounding, role-playing, puppetry, painting, talking. Release of toxic content is of paramount importance since cups full of anger, hate, gloom, and de-spair cannot be filled with tolerance, love, joy, and hope. The full cup must first be emptied.

Emptying. In an atmosphere of trust children are reassured they can be open to their feelings, they can be aware of what they are ex-periencing. We ask them to accurately report and communicate their frustration. We encourage them by asking questions and by drawing them out. We listen with empathy. We try to understand and help all the children comprehend what is happening inside and outside of them-selves. We don't give advice. We mostly listen.

Filling. We realize we must go beyond catharsis (emptying) to un-derstanding and action. We ask the children to thoughtfully consider the consequences of their behavior. (After their feelings have been honored rather than denied, they are usually willing to think further about their situation.) We feel this feedback of how their emotion and behavior affects themselves and others is important data for them to consider.

Then they are asked to choose from among their thought-out list of

---

[2]Jourard, Sidney, *Disclosing Man To Himself*, Van Nostrand Reinhold, New York, 1968, p. 167.

alternatives those which they can translate into action with committment and consistency. Support is given at this time to help them achieve their goal. They are urged to ask for any help that might strengthen and undergird their committment to responsible action. As they assume responsibility, they find others capable of love and response to them.

Validation and values clarification groups with the children meet each week to continue the search for self-identity and values. The strategies that follow have been used successfully in these groups. The authors believe with Abe Maslow that ". . . it is possible that we may soon define therapy as a search for values, because ultimately the search for identity is, in essence, the search for ones own, intrinsic, authentic values."[3]

A BIT OF THEORY

Before his death in 1970, Abe Maslow wrote, ". . . the function of education, the goal of education—the human goal, the humanistic goal, the goal so far as human beings are concerned—is ultimately the 'self-actualization' of a person, the becoming fully human, the development of the fullest height that the human species can stand up to or that the particular individual can come to. In a less technical way, it is helping the person to become the best that he is able to become."[4] He viewed ". . . learning one's identity as an essential part of education. If education doesn't do that, it is useless. Education is learning to grow, learning what to grow toward, learning what is good and bad, learning what is desirable and understandable, learning what to choose and what not to choose."[5]

Throughout our book we offer opportunities for children to grow, each day to become the best they are capable of being. Growth is a day-by-day process—gradual—slow—continuous. There are no shortcuts. Abe Maslow thought that children "don't live for the sake of far goals or for the distant future. They are living not preparing to live."[6] He questioned how growth came about and answered it simply ". . . growth takes place when the next step forward is subjectively more

[3]Maslow, A. H., *Toward A Psychology of Being*, Van Nostrand Reinhold, New York, 1968, p. 177.
[4]Maslow, A. H., *The Farther Reaches of Human Nature*, Viking Press, New York, 1971, p. 169.
[5]Ibid., p. 179.
[6]Maslow, *Toward A Psychology of Being*, 1968, p. 44.

delightful, more joyous, more intrinsically satisfying than the previous gratification with which we have become familiar and even bored . . ."[7] You will find in our strategies and activities invitations to grow, to explore, experience, choose, delight, enjoy "in a serendipitous way."[8] The strategies are designed to produce growth by lessening the fears of growing and making it a delightful experience, two valences that Maslow thought of as "growth-through-delight." He had great faith in people-kind to choose what was best for them . . . "if free choice is really free and the chooser is not too sick or frightened to choose, he will choose wisely, in a healthy and growthful direction, more often than not."[9]

Maslow devised a theory of human motivation which we have attempted to translate in practical, down-to-earth strategies for children. He felt, as we do, that "Human needs arrange themselves in hierarchies of pre-potency. That is to say, the appearance of one need usually rests on the prior satisfaction of another more pre-potent need. Man is a perpetually wanting animal . . ."[10]

Maslow wrote of basic needs. First, the physiological needs, essentially the need for food. "A creature that has never had a full stomach is incapable of conceiving of any other need and conversely, is incapable of realizing that the satisfaction of the need for food would not lead to a state of permanent bliss."[11] We meet the hunger needs of our children with full cupboards and refrigerator. If our children are hungry when they arrive at school, milk and cereal is provided. We routinely provide "juice break" and "relaxation time" each morning. At noon we prepare our own lunch with the help of the children who become the menu-planners, bakers, cooks, waiters, waitresses, and cleanup crew. Children are always free to go to the water fountain and rest rooms. In these simple ways we meet the most basic need of children. We realize this rather complete food service plan is not possible for all schools but simple modifications can be made for children to eat a bowl of cereal, enjoy a juice break, relax and later enjoy a hot lunch. By removing the obsession for food, a child is more free to learn.

When hunger is satisfied, the safety needs emerge—"the need for freedom from pain or fear, the need for a regular routine that will give a sense of a predictable orderly world."[12] We provide this regularity with our daily schedule:[13]

---

[7]Ibid, p. 45.
[8]Ibid, p. 45.
[9]Ibid, p. 48.
[10]Wilson, Colin, *New Pathways in Psychology*, New American Library, New York, 1972, p. 147.
[11]Ibid, p. 148.
[12]Ibid, p. 148.
[13]For a full description of our daily schedule see *Appendix*, "Programming for Troubled Children."

9:00– 9:15   Love and Care
9:15– 9:30   Body Awakening
9:30–10:00   Story Time
10:00–10:20 Free Play
10:20–11:20 Head Tripping
11:20–11:30 Please Touch
11:30–12:30 Lunch and Recess
12:30– 2:00 Projects
2:00– 2:15   Sharing Time
2:20–   Going Home

"Much of the child's world is being modified daily, and he learns that he needs some routine in order to provide a degree of stability around which change can freely occur. Many advocates of 'free schools' or 'creative schools' thought they were doing a service to their children by abolishing all schedules and routines. However it was observed that abolishing schedules caused a marked rise in frustration and acting out, negative behavior."[14] All schools have their own schedules and routines which provide children with a sense of security. With a few adaptations these same schedules can provide for variety, excitement, and human needs.

In the following pages we offer other suggestions for meeting the safety needs of children. The chapters on *Self Disclosure–Authenticity, Feelings–Emotions, Touching–Validating* are particularly pertinent.

Love needs are next to emerge. "A person with a fair degree of security . . . with a stable place of abode . . . now begins to feel keenly the need for friends . . . for a place in his group."[15] This need for love involves both the giving and receiving of love. There is much overlapping of love in all of our strategies. We intend for love to permeate each activity but we suggest the sections on *Love*, on *Touching*, and on *Validating and Parent Involvement* as especially designed to meet the increased need for love.

As the love needs are satisfied the needs of esteem emerge, ". . . the need for a stable, firmly based, high evaluation of self, for self-respect . . . and for the esteem of others."[16] Our chapter on *Freedom to Learn* and *Values Clarification Strategies* helps meet the children's needs for mastery and competence in various tasks and skills that enable them to deserve the praise of others. Each teacher can again consider the individual abilities of children and assign tasks that are neither too easy nor too hard.

[14]Read, Donald A. and Sidney B. Simon, *Humanistic Education Sourcebook*, Prentice-Hall, Englewood Cliffs, New Jersey, 1975, p. 335 from "Educational Applications of Humanistic Psychology" by Dennis Romig and Chas. C. Cleland.
[15]Wilson, Colin, *New Pathways in Psychology*, p. 148.
[16]Ibid, p. 148.

Finally, at the top of the hierarchy is the need for "self-actualization," "to become everything that one is capable of becoming."[17] Although Maslow felt that only about 1 percent of our population actually achieves this goal, we feel all children need experiences that anticipate this high level of functioning. We have provided the chapter *Strategies for Giving Meaning to Life* for this purpose because, as Maslow pointed out, ". . . life has to have meaning, has to be filled with moments of high intensity that validate life and make it worthwhile. Otherwise the desire to die makes sense, for who would want to endure endless pain or endless boredom?"[18]

Because there is so much overlap in all of these strategies, we have not ordered them sequentially but have trusted in the classroom teacher's judgment in integrating and relating the strategies to his or her particular educational plan and to the individual needs of those children being taught.

A NOTE TO TEACHERS

We have some very practical, down-to-earth goals. We want each of our children at Boxelder School to feel important, cared for, listened to, and loved as people who are learning to extend themselves in loving ways. We work hard to reduce failure, fear, and hatred for school, and to substitute instead more personal growth, intimacy, and happiness. These good things happen with children when teachers care as much about nurturing healthy self-respect in their students as they do about educating them.

Every one of our children has a learning problem that is either organic or emotional in nature. They have been variously described as "difficult to reach," "uncontrollable," or "outside the reach of the normal classroom." They come to regard themselves as "stupid," "dumb," "weird," "crazy," "creepy." In this book we offer strategies designed to counter these feelings of failure, shame, and fear and to enhance creative growth and feelings of love.

At Boxelder we treat troubled, difficult, failure-oriented children, but we recommend the strategies of this book as preventive measures as well as corrective ones. We have used these methods with "normal" children in "regular classrooms." With these children the activities are regarded as joyful experiences. We find their responses to be richer,

[17]Ibid, p. 149.
[18]Maslow, *The Farther Reaches of Human Nature,* 1971, p. 188.

more inciteful than those of the difficult child. But this again is a function of their own mental and emotional development. Most of the strategies do not require a child to read or write and can be used with "slow" and "retarded" children. Too many children among those who are not regarded as "difficult" feel helpless, confused and angry often at a very early age. Even by first grade many cannot separate "I'm not very good at reading (or writing or arithmetic)" from "I'm not very good!" So much of how they behave grows out of negative self-esteem and continues to prove to them how bad they really are.

We designed this to be a book "for all seasons" and "for most kids," normal, slow-learning, retarded, emotionally disturbed, and learning disabled. (We have not attempted the strategies with gifted, deaf, or severely retarded youngsters.) In our experience we have discovered no contraindications from any of the strategies included here. We have "thrown out" many strategies over the two year period this book has been in production because they did not excite or motivate students. The strategies we retained for you are ones that "click" and "work" well. All of the activities involve children in what is going on around them and help them feel that in some way they have a part in shaping their own future. Values clarification, validation, and humanistic methods are ways to inject into the educational setting opportunities for children to think, choose, affirm, and act with feelings of success, thus learning a process that can guide them the rest of their lives.

Slowly the children at Boxelder learned to come out of the deep, dark hiding places within themselves. Their attempts were slight at first—a gesture, a word, an expressed feeling now and then—but slowly they trusted enough to present small parts of themselves. And their attempts were received with warmth, encouragement, and above all, acceptance.[19]

As our children grow so do we the authors. Children who are developing-learning are our greatest validation! We learn from your feedback too and we invite your response. If you create an activity or embellish one of ours, we would appreciate your sharing it with us. This book is only a beginning. We fantasize and hope for future revisions, additions, and new publications. If we use any of your ideas they will be gratefully acknowledged. Please send your ideas to

Robert O'Rourke
3809 Crescent Drive
Fort Collins, Colorado 80521

---

[19]Many of the above ideas were adapted from Simon, Sidney and Robert O'Rourke, "Every Child Has High Worth," *Learning*, Dec. 1975, pp. 46–50.

TWO

self disclosure-- authenticity

Both Carl Rogers and Sidney Jourard have cherished the qualities of openness and realness. Carl Rogers spoke of these qualities as one of the most important things he had learned in his life time. He said, "In my relationships with a person I have found that it does not help, in the long run, to act as though I were something I am not. . . . I have not found it helpful or effective . . . to try to maintain a facade, to act in one way on the surface when I am experiencing something quite different underneath."[1] At the margin of the book where Carl wrote these words one of the authors had added, years ago, "Carl has found it doesn't help to be phoney! He believes in being authentic!"

Sidney Jourard felt that being real, visible, and transparent was part of being mentally healthy. He felt it essential to mental well-being to be . . . "fully known to at least one other significant human being."[2] He proposed that people might seek psychological help ". . . because they have not disclosed themselves in some optimum degree to the people in their life."[3]

To Jourard it was imperative to be real and to be known, ". . . it is not until I am my real self and I act my real self that my real self is in a position to grow. One's self grows from the consequence of being. People's selves stop growing when they repress them."[4] He summarizes his view with this statement, "Every maladjusted person is a person who has not made himself known to another human being and in consequence does not know himself."[5]

We have provided opportunities for our children to experience their real selves in the following selected strategies:

1. Getting to Know You (teacher and student experiment with self-disclosure, being known)
2. Show and Tell (what children think and care about)
3. Telegrams—Viewpoints (being open and also learning about the concealed, projected self)
4. Public Interview (how we live and what we believe)
5. Survival Kit (candid opinions about school)

---

[1] Rogers, Carl R., *On Becoming A Person,* Houghton Mifflin, Boston, 1961, pp. 16–17.
[2] Jourard, Sidney M., *The Transparent Self,* Van Nostrand Reinhold, New York, 1964, p. 25.
[3] Ibid, p. 21.
[4] Ibid, p. 25.
[5] Ibid, p. 26.

6. Autobiography (discovering the importance of telling personal events from individual life stories)
7. The Meaning of My Name (developing an identity through the personal meanings of my name)

The above strategies help set a direction for children to follow to discover an identity. By discovering an identity we mean, "... finding out what our real desires and characteristics are, and being able to live in a way that expresses them. You learn to be authentic, to be honest ... most of us have learned to avoid authenticity ... authenticity is the reduction of phoniness toward the zero point."[6] Authenticity is important for both teacher and learner if growth is to happen. Facades block truth, honesty, and spontaneous expression. These few strategies are beginnings to help teachers and children become aware of who they are and how they really react to others by giving them a chance to tell what's going on inside of them instead of being devious, defensive, and evasive.

STRATEGY NO. 1 ───────────────────────
getting to know you

When Anna was called to the small country of Siam to teach the King's children she thought it was essential "to get to know" the children at an intimate level before she started teaching them. "Getting to know all about them" was Anna's way of caring—her way of prizing each child as a unique individual; so they talked, sang songs together, and learned to trust.

Children are also eager to know their teacher on more human terms—to experience the authenticity, the being, the aliveness of their teacher. They hope for a teacher who is not afraid of being visible and real, who can say to them with quiet dignity, "I'm searching for values and a better way of life every day also and I'll be glad to share some of the discoveries I've made, some things I believe in now. I don't expect you to follow me or adopt my beliefs; I offer my thoughts as a gift, as alternatives for you to consider. Real learning happens when you experience and discover for yourselves."

We offer these first values clarification strategies as possible approaches to becoming real, honest human beings to your students.

[6]Maslow, A. H., *The Farther Reaches of Human Nature*, The Viking Press, New York, 1971, p. 183.

Perhaps they will help reduce the mystery that sometimes exists between teacher and student and will promote the search for learning.

Write on a sheet of paper fifteen things you love to do. This is one way to discover what makes life most satisfying and meaningful for you.

Go over your list and choose three loves that you feel are the most important and simply talk for a few minutes to your class about these priorities in your life. An interesting way to present this small segment of your life is to make a collage portraying these three loves or to use illustrations shown on an overhead projector.

After you have talked about the things, objects, and people whom you most love, invite your students to interview you. This provides another opportunity for them to know you as a person on a more intimate level. Then ask the group to write a series of sentences beginning with:

I learned_____.

I wish_____.

I was happy that_____ .

I wonder_____ .

I was surprised that_____.

Each student is asked to volunteer one or two statements from the above discoveries. Students who do not wish to share their ideas are always given the option to pass. Only in this way can you hope to build trust. Gradually throughout the year most of your students will learn to share and become involved and when they do it is because they chose freely to do so.

If your students seem interested in modeling your behavior and sharing their lives with the class, use this same strategy on successive days with one student each day as a focus person.

Sidney Jourard, teacher-psychologist, has posed two questions:

"How can I love a person whom I do not know?"

"How can a person love me if he does not know me?"[7]

We hope these simple strategies will achieve two goals. First, they will help reduce the psychological distance that sometimes exists between teacher and student. Second, through the use of these techniques a more personal I-thou relationship is achieved as a basis for more effective learning.

[7]Jourard, *The Transparent Self,* 1964, p. 25.

Ask yourself this question: "What teachers in my life have really made a difference?" We suspect you will remember those for whom you have felt affection. Through these teachers you learned something about real life and living. You learned because they cared about you; with them your education was not so much a matter of the mind as of the heart.

STRATEGY NO. 2 ———————————————————————

show and tell

When we remember school, teachers, classes, and first grade, we recall a circle of children showing and telling about things they valued. Show and Tell was a powerful, simple, happy way to affirm those things we prized most. After the first grade the technique was abruptly dropped, probably because we had to get on with learning more formal facts (mind over heart again—intellect over emotion) an emphasis on knowing more than caring.

Show and Tell considers personal values—what children care about—how they live—what they think. We use Show and Tell with all ages, children through adults, as a strategy to affirm and clarify values. Simply ask your group to bring something they would like to share either by telling or showing with the group. We ask each child to limit the presentation to three minutes so that all will have an opportunity to talk. At the end of the session we quickly move around the group, stopping with each child for a moment to ask any questions the group wishes to pursue in regard to the presentation.

Our children have shared Mickey Mouse hats and trips to California, a thumb nail that "came off" after a door was slammed on it, a sleeping bag, a dump truck, a teddy bear, rocks, a billy goat, a necklace, and an airplane that flew with a string. Behind each article was a memory, a smile or a tear, an affection, something of value, something of self; each perhaps as important as the geography of Brazil, forms of a verb, or 9 times 9.

STRATEGY NO. 3 ————————————————————————

telegrams: I urge . . .
viewpoints: children are . . .

There is a psychological principle that says simply: Much of what we are and what we believe gets projected onto other people and things. The statement *"You* really appear tired today" may, in reality, convey something about the person making the observation. He or she may be projecting and, in truth, saying, *"I* am really tired today." "I urge you to tickle yourself more and have more fun" may really mean "I wish I could let down my hair, relax, and enjoy more." The principle of projection is interesting and applicable to people—adults as well as children—in clarifying needs and values.

An interesting strategy is to encourage children to send brief "I Urge Telegrams." Because our children have difficulty with writing we send brief messages of 20 words or less by personal contact or by tape recording. With the children in a circle we ask them to send an "I Urge Telegram" to anyone in the group. The person receiving the message is asked to consider the request and accept the message if it is reasonable. If the receiver feels the urging is inappropriate, he or she may respond briefly, as honestly and responsibly as possible. We do not feel long dialog or debate is especially helpful in this strategy. The essence of the technique is to provide a simple activity whereby students can state briefly and clearly beliefs they have thoughtfully considered and which they hope will be accepted with a response to action.

"I Urge Telegrams" have been written by our children to their teachers and to parents, as well as to friends. At this point they have not reached out to government officials, celebrities, or others outside of school. We incorporate the idea with good results in the Sharing Circle Strategy, page 102.

We use another group activity in which for three or four minutes we ask the children to discuss the sentence stem, "Children are basically _____. We ask the children to state their beliefs about children in general with some evidence as to why they believe their statement is accurate and valid.

We then ask them to think about all the statements that were made about children, especially those personal statements made by each child. Then each is asked to change the statement from

"Children are basically_____" to

"I am basically____._____"

We use this technique, not to trick or trap the children, but to bring them to the realization that much of what we urge others to do we want for ourselves and much of what we might say about another person may well reflect how we feel about ourselves.

These illustrate some of the telegrams sent:

Dear Mom: I wish you'd let me go outside and play more.

Dear Dad: Don't yell and cuss at me when I do wrong. Just tell me when I do wrong.

Dear Mom: I want to join the Boy Scouts.

Dear Mom: Let me hang posters in my room.

Dear Teachers: We want more recess and longer lunch hours.

Dear Teachers: Why don't you help us wash dishes sometimes?

Dear Teachers: Don't give us so much work.

Dear Teachers: Give us more art and wood time.

Dear Friends: Why don't you come over to my house more? I always have to go to your house.

Dear Friend: Tell me if I do something you don't like.

Dear Friend: Play with me more.

In response to the sentence stem, "Children are basically_____, the children said "Children are basically 'good,' 'people,' 'retarded,' 'don't do what you tell them,' 'cool,' 'intelligent,' 'kind,' 'nice,' 'helpful,' 'mean,' and 'bad'!"

STRATEGY NO. 4 ——————————————————
public interview (our family)

The Public Interview has long been a part of the values clarification strategies because it is so adaptable to the many areas where students experience confusion and conflict. Some of these areas are:

family	school
friends	rules
vocation	money
sex	

We chose one topic, the family, as a focus because with most children there are many conflicting value issues within this primary group.

To begin, we ask all the children to close their eyes and bring to mind a mental picture of their mothers and then quickly, remember her saying something to them. We ask the children to hold this in their mind while they do the same with their fathers: "What do they hear their fathers say?"

We then go around the circle asking the children to repeat the sentences they heard their fathers and mothers say ("Wash your hands," "Eat everything on your plate," "Always be a good boy," "Let's go fishing," all reflect values of a sort), and, of course, a child is always given the option to pass.

As a second activity we ask the children to draw their families and then make up a story about them of not more than seven or eight lines in length. These stories are told to the group. After this discussion we allow children to ask each other questions about their particular family as a way of acquainting themselves with the beliefs, values, and actions of various families.

As a last strategy we ask for volunteers and pose the following questions to the children who consent to be interviewed:

1. What are some things you talk about in your family?
2. What are some things you feel you need to talk about?
3. What names are you called in your family by your parents, brothers, and sisters?
4. How is your family helpful to you?
5. In what ways do you think they are harmful to you?
6. How would you improve your family life?
7. What contributions do you make to your family?
8. Would you like to have a family someday? What kind of family would you have?
9. If you could choose your family from this group, who would you include? Give reasons why.

Children's Reactions

The topics of family discussion were as follows:

"We talk about my pets and how I need to take care of them."

"We don't talk much. We just sit around watching T.V."

"Mom likes to talk about her plants, especially her fern."

There were needs the children felt should be discussed:

"I'd like to talk about how I feel about going back to regular school."

"I want to talk about moving out of the ol' trailer house into a real house."

"I'd like to talk with dad about getting the old rocking chair he had when he was a kid. I would like to fix it up and rock in it."

We expected nicknames, many times a form of endearment, to be used between members of the family, but most of the children interviewed were called by their given names: one was called "son," another "sonny," others were called "Mr." and "kook."

Family "helpfulness" was seen in the following ways:

"They clean my room."

"They buy my clothes."

"My mother gives me pills when I need them." (a hyperactive boy)

"They give us food."

"They remind me to carry out the trash."

When asked "Are your families ever harmful to you?" there was complete denial.

The only way most of the children felt they could improve family life was to "work harder and help more around the house." Our children "help" their families by "doing dishes," "taking out the trash," "cleaning my room," "throwing the dirty clothes in the hamper," and "not bugging dad when he comes home from work."

Most of the children interviewed aspired to have a family, one that was "happy," "clean," with "not many kids."

A nine year old boy portrays his family:

The first figure drawn was the brother who is cutting the lawn (Tim sees his brother as a cutting person). Tim said his brother had run over him and shot him in the air calling for "help!" In answer, his brother says, "huh?" as if unable to hear or care about Tim being "mowed down."

The father is drawn next, small and in the background. The father is also mowing the lawn (another cutting person), but the lawn mower according to Tim is "out of control." Big drops of perspiration flow from the father as he tries desperately to gain control. (The father is ineffective in the home situation and frantically attempts control.) The house is small and distant which, we feel, indicates that Tim feels quite apart and separated from his home.

The mother first appeared at 1 but was erased. She was then placed at 2 on top of the house. Finally she was placed above the house on a plane "heading south." (It is as if Tim had a premonition his mother would soon leave the family. She did so four months after the drawing was completed. The separation ended in divorce.) Perhaps this is why Tim had such difficulty in placing her in his family drawing in the first place. She had ceased to "belong" as part of the family.

Tim is seen to the far right of the picture coming home from school. He yells, "Hi dad, what's for supper?" (It is interesting that the question is directed to the father to whom Tim looks for nurture.)

STRATEGY NO. 5
survival kit

The story is told of Ernest Hemingway that he was once interviewed about his career in writing and was asked if there wasn't one essential ingredient that makes a great writer. Hemingway replied, "Yes there is. In order to be a great writer a person must have a built-in shockproof crap detector."

Our children have no such detection device, which many times must leave them at the mercy of their environment. Their survival, especially in the regular school where most met with rejection, was always in jeopardy, so we began to think of their ability to cope—their ability to survive in this milieu—and we came up with the idea of a Survival Kit. We asked them, "What does it take to survive a day in the regular school? What would you put in a Survival Kit that would help you?" We thought that after all of their experienced frustration and failure they were especially kind.

Some of their responses were:

"You sure need lots of patience."

"Chewing gum would help."

and

"Long breaks at recess and lunch."

We are including this short strategy because we thought other teachers might like to learn from their classes what it takes for each child to survive one day of school. It might be one way to determine students' willingness to be self-disclosing.

STRATEGY NO. 6 ——————————————————————————
autobiography

Sidney Jourard wrote, "Through my self-disclosure, I let others know my soul. They can know it, really know it only as I make it known. In fact I am beginning to suspect that I can't even know my own soul except as I disclose it. I suspect that I will know myself 'for real' at the exact moment that I have succeeded in making it known through my disclosure to another person."[8] Even more emphatically he continues, "Every maladjusted person is a person who has not made himself known to another being and in consequence does not know himself."[9]

We offer our children a safe environment for self-disclosure through their autobiographies. We begin at a comfortable level asking the children in group to simply discuss their favorite food, movie, book, musical group, city, toy, television program, hobby, sport, color, etc. In this first go-round children discover how much they are really alike.

Then to discover uniqueness and individuality, we ask for a discussion of more personal material. We ask each child to select one topic and discuss it with a trusted person in the group. The first person talks for three minutes while the other person listens without interruption. Then the listening person has three minutes of uninterrupted telling. At the end of the six minutes each person thinks of one strength that has been discovered about the partner and tells this person in one sentence of personal validation. After the validation all of the pairs return to the group and share their discovery of strength about their partners. Some topics for self-disclosure include:

> A turning point in your life when you changed quite drastically.
> Who have been the people in your life who taught you the most? What did they teach that you feel is important?
> Friends I have had in my life—what they meant to me—what we did together, etc.
> Pets I have enjoyed.

[8]Jourard, *The Transparent Self,* 1968, p. 10.
[9]Ibid, p. 26.

What places have you lived? Why did you move from each place?

Explain the most important problem facing you today.

What were some of the high and low points of last year?

What have been some of your greatest achievements so far in life?

List some of your most difficult times so far.

What do you think you would like to do when you finish school?

What are some jobs or occupations you once thought would be interesting?

Sidney Harris, journalist, once wrote, "The personality . . . is not an apple that has to be polished, but a banana that has to be peeled." In his column he went on to say that most people spend their time in polishing a role they want others to perceive rather than removing this polished facade that conceals the real, authentic person. So long as we hide behind peelings we can never hope to have any meaningful encounter with others.

STRATEGY NO. 7

the meaning of my name

Nothing is more individual than a person's own name. Since the beginning of time, every human being has been identified by at least one name. In references such as dictionaries and encyclopedias common and uncommon names are given with their individual meanings.

Florence = flower (Latin)

Charles = manly (old German)

Philip = lover of horses (Greek)

Esther = star (Persian)[10]

None of our children knew the personal meanings of their names so we researched each one and made them each a name tag with the personal meaning printed on it.

Then we asked them why they thought their parents might have named them what they did. Did they like their name and meaning? We asked the group "In what ways, for example, is Florence "like a flower," Charles, "manly?" We then asked them about their other names. Middle names? Meanings? What are their nicknames? Why? Is their "nickname"

[10]*The World Book Encyclopedia,* Vol. 12, Field Enterprises Educational Corporation, Chicago, 1958, p. 5378.

more appropriate than their "given" name? Why? Would they like to change their name and the meaning of it? Does their last name (surname) have meaning? (Shoemaker, Potter, Carpenter, John*son*, etc.) Would they like to change these names? We asked them all to assume a new name by printing their first names backwards so that "Tom" became "Mot." Then we asked them what "Mot" could stand for? The children then brainstormed meanings. "Mot means:

"strength"

"good"

"the big one"

"chief"

(We made ground rules that all the meanings must be complimentary and in some way reflective of the way they saw the person.)

If the child chose to remain "Mot" and accept that word as his nickname the other children agreed that "Mot he would be," and we christened him "Mot, the Chief—full of strength and goodness."

In this simple way our children learned the meaning of their names as one source of pride and identity. If they wanted to project a newer, more imaginative view of themselves, this was permitted. Perhaps everyone at some time in their life should have the opportunity to discard old names for newer ones. As a followup activity we asked each child to draw a symbol that would visually represent their name. We then gave them several popular examples:

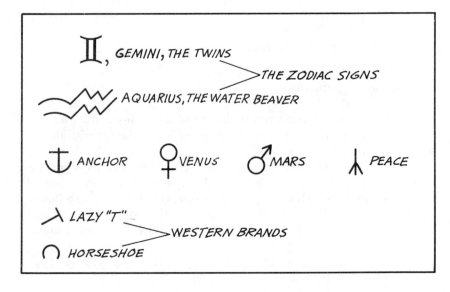

The children then explained what their personal symbols meant. Each symbol was then made into a poster and placed above the child's personal study booth to show private ownership.

We chose the following symbols to illustrate some of the children's responses:

"A basketball and football would mean I'm trying to be a good sport." (A boy, age 11)

"My symbol is an eagle and it stands for strength." (A boy, age 10)

"A flower could mean peaceful. I like a flower." (A girl, age 9)

"A sun is the symbol that means being happy." (A girl, age 7)

THREE

---

strategies for giving meaning to life

---

we all need dreams

peak experiences

freeway

living courageously

because we are human

a quiet spot

a place for me

Victor Frankl, one of Europe's most respected psychotherapists, developed most of his ideas in a German concentration camp in World War II. He, like Abraham Maslow, mainly worked alone; yet their ideas are quite similar. Frankl's thinking perhaps can be summarized by three of his major insights:

1. "In order to feel fully alive, a man needs goals in the future."[1] Frankl felt that without future goals people were simply marking time and barely existing.
2. He felt also that this purposive stance depends more on a person's attitude than on actual, definite goals. Future purpose gives the individual the optimism, the energy, and the desire to live.
3. "Meaning sets the pace of being. Existence falters unless it is lived in terms of transcendence beyond itself."[2]

Much of Maslow's work emphasized what he called "peak-experiences," those wonderful, happy, ecstatic moments when all of life seems thrillingly alive. He saw in those experiences the essence of life, being, and identity. He wrote: (1) "All the peak-experiences are . . . integrative of the splits within the person, between persons, within the world, and between the person and the world. Since one aspect of health is integration, the peak-experiences are moves toward health and are themselves momentary healths; (2) These experiences are life validating, i.e., they make life worth while . . . ; (3) They are worthwhile in themselves. . . ."[3]

Both Frankl and Maslow sought to arouse a renewed interest in life, to encourage people to look for something beyond themselves, to hope. Since we feel this optimism is especially important for children, we have designed six experiences that go beyond or transcend their present existence. Some of these validate their present existence. We feel both experiences are necessary, being in the present with optimism for tomorrow.

1. We All Need Dreams (life does need strong ideas and ideals or it is meaningless)

[1] Wilson, Colin, *New Pathways in Psychology*, New American Library, New York, 1972, p. 192.
[2] Ibid, p. 193.
[3] Maslow, Abraham H., *Toward a Psychology of Being*, Van Nostrand Reinhold, New York, 1968, p. 210.

2. Peak Experiences (dipping into the past—remembering and validating life as being good)
3. Freeway (life—planning—decisions for future living)
4. Living Courageously (an affirmation that children can act courageously and with confidence)
5. Because We Are Human (life is and holds the possibility for fascination)
6. A Quiet Spot (relaxing and feeling good in a now experience with roots in the past)
7. A Place for Me (design for a nourishing environment)

We agree with Maslow: "One of the goals of education should be to teach that life is precious."[4] If there were no joy in life, it would not be worth living. It is through dreams, peak experiences, being deeply human, and recalling joyful memories that our children relearn life-affirmation.

STRATEGY NO. 1 —————————————————————————

we all need dreams

In the Broadway play, "South Pacific," wise old Mary sings about "talking happy." She advocates "talking about things you like to do. . . ." She remembers from her own life watching a bird learning to fly, silent stars peeping through trees, a silver moon floating in the sky, and the ripples of the sea. She concludes that ". . . you've got to have a dream—If you don't have a dream—How you gonna make a dream come true?"

We use these ideas of happy talk and realizing dreams with our children because they are based on psychological positions that both Abe Maslow and Victor Frankl asserted when they talked and wrote about life needing strong ideals, something beyond the self, the things that give meaning to existence.

There are times when we pair each child with someone they would like to be with for ten minutes and we ask them to "talk happy," to remember a "happy thing" from their last few weeks of living. They take turns, one listening for five minutes, one talking. Later we call them back to the larger group and ask for volunteers to tell about their partner's happy experience. We then play "Happy Talk" from *South Pacific* to set the mood for the next exercise: dreams.

In our second activity we ask the children to leave the present time,

[4]Maslow, Abraham H., *The Farther Reaches of Human Nature*, New York: The Viking Press, Inc., 1971, p. 187.

which for most of them, is rather empty. We invite them to transcend time and space and imagine their hopes for the future: Where would they like to be when they "grow up"? What would they like to be doing? What would they be feeling? What things and people would they have around them? The children then close their eyes and dream of their futures. In their dreams they drive big powerful semi-trucks across the continent, live on peaceful farms surrounded by animals, and all-in-all recapture the idea that life is worthwhile and there is hope!

STRATEGY NO. 2

peak experiences

One part of validation is remembering the good times in life. Abe Maslow viewed these good times as "peak experiences" when people really felt more "together," joyful, peaceful and happy, at the zenith of their power; a time when things came easy and life was enjoyable.

This strategy enables children to recall times in their lives when they were thoroughly happy, feeling good, and having fun. We interviewed the children individually and asked them to recall a peak experience in their lives. As they talked, we wrote down the details and later collected the ideas into short paragraphs. We asked each child not to reveal the story to the other children, because we would later read it to the group to see if anyone could guess who told the story.

We met for our regular weekly group and read each child's story. After the children guessed who told the story we asked, "From hearing this story, what would you say   (Name of Child)   values in life?" We then listed on newsprint all of the values symbolized by the individual stories. Below are a few examples:

> "I remember a time when I was about five or six years old and we visited my grandmother in the summertime. She lived out by California on a desert. They caught me a horse and I rode him out on the desert all by myself. It was my first time to ever be in the desert and I saw wild squirrels and lots of birds. It was also the first time I'd ever ridden a horse and that's what made me feel so happy." (Girl—Values: independence, adventure, harmony with nature)

> "My happiest time was on my mother's birthday when I was about nine years old. Me and dad made her a cake and we all bought her presents. We saved up a lot of money and us kids got her Avon perfume that you rub on. Dad got her a dress and a new hat. I was really excited. I felt like crying and laughing at the same time." (Boy—Values: family, giving–sharing)

"My happiest time was today when me and Billy was playing in the tunnel, hiding from the other kids. Billy wasn't upset and I could play with him. That was fun for me." (Boy— Values: peace, joy, understanding)

The aftermath of a peak experience is also felt to have therapeutic value in that the recall brings clarification, validation, and insight into our presence in the world.

In the following areas the "aftermath" is complementary to the process of value clarification:

1. People may come to a more healthy view of themselves.
2. They may view others in a more positive way.
3. They may see their world as a better place to live.
4. They may seek to repeat the peak experience since it was so delightful to them.
5. They may feel that life is worthwhile, exciting, and beautiful.

Throughout the following weeks the children may want to keep a log of their good times; seeing in this way if they can increase the number of peak experiences in their lives. (For more about peak experiences, you might read Maslow's book, *Toward a Psychology of Being*, Chap. 6 and 7.)

STRATEGY NO. 3 —————————————————————————

freeway

Life can be looked upon as a freeway. Up ahead are the destinations of a life and all along the way are exits. Some of the exits are necessary and important while others are unseemly and dangerous. Children need to be made aware of the important exits that leave the freeway for awhile but lead back to the main thoroughfare resulting in a happy, productive life. They also need to understand the exits that may lead down back roads to roadblocks and hazardous deadends.

We gave the children freeway maps and asked them to describe exits that hold potential for making the journey of life more exciting and rewarding—perhaps education, recreation, and meaningful work. We asked them to get in touch with exits that are inappropriate detours —perchance drugs, dropping out of school, a bad marriage, etc. Each child then individualized the freeway map with personalized exits to enhance the journey and with ramps to be avoided. This helps insure that this freeway is, in the words of Carlos Castaneda, ". . . a path with a heart."

Then we asked the children to close their eyes and fantasize where they would like to be along the freeway in ten years, what would they be doing, what feelings would they have, what relationships, what things would they own, how do they plan to achieve these things? We asked them to "be there" for a time, feeling their experience, being a part of it, via the highway of daydreams.

Abe Maslow wrote with great wisdom about the choices each of us makes in life. "Every crime against one's own nature, every evil act, every one without exception records itself in our unconscious and makes us despise ourselves . . . it registers. If we do something we are ashamed of it registers to our discredit and if we do something honest or fine or good it registers to our credit. The net results ultimately are either one or the other—either we respect and accept ourselves or we despise ourselves and feel contemptible, worthless and unlovable."[5]

We have included one of our children's illustrations of what his personal "freeway of life" would include, along with his fantasy of how he would like his life ordered in future years. It shows how one child responded to the stimulus of the "Freeway Strategy" and how, through his considerations, reflections, and fantasies, he expressed himself through action-by-drawing. Group discussion further helps children in clarifying these concepts included in life planning.

This child thought he could achieve this dream if he "kept on practicing basketball and went out each year for the team" and if he "lifted weights; took vitamins (especially 'C') and ate good food." "I'd also have to finish high school and college so that means hard studying."

This same boy fantasized that in ten years he would "like to be a professional basketball player," who lived "in the mountains" and had a house, dog, and Corvette" and "probably a wife."

---

[5] Maslow, *Toward a Psychology of Being*, 1968, p. 5.

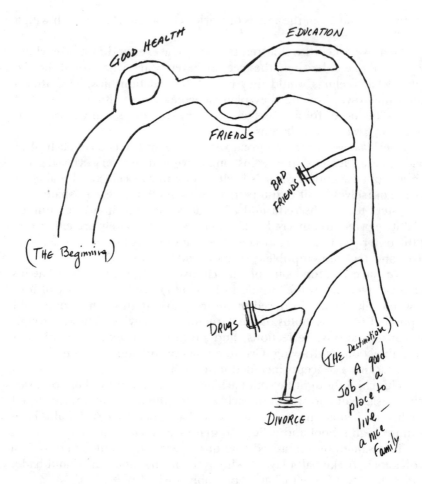

STRATEGY NO. 4 ————————————————————
living courageously

Courage: What is it? Where do you get it? Do you have it? How have you acted courageously? These questions help children examine and inventory their lives for moments of greatness and strength. Children who have not conquered, not overcome fear, and not withstood adversity feel doubtful that they can. Recalling a courageous action can change a child's self-concept in the direction of strength.

To introduce the strategy we ask the children to respond briefly to the above four questions in order to get a feel of what constitutes courage. We then read a poignant story from the June, 1974 issue of *Reader's Digest* about a heroic kitten, Marco, who overcame blindness and continued to live fearlessly. This small animal, described by the author, Era Zistel, as a "peerless teacher," further defines what it means to live courageously despite *handicaps*. (Some described our children as emotionally *handicapped*.) So this simple story is compelling and forceful in it's impact.

During the week following the story each child was interviewed and asked to tell about a time in his or her life that showed some spirit or daring. Each child's story was outlined by the teacher and the child was instructed to keep the courageous act a secret until the next group meeting. In the intervening time each child's story was typed on a 4 × 8 card.

When the group met again each secret story was read from the card and the children attempted to guess which one in the group had performed each particular brave action.

Two followup activities helped the children give further consideration to courage:

1. During a short discussion period we talked about:
   a. Times when you have seen other people do things which you consider courageous.
      Our children told us of one child who was constantly being bullied by an older student at a bus stop. The child, they thought, acted courageously by "punching the bully in the face." The child who confronted his antagonist responded, "And you helped by standing by me."
      One child had heard the story of the chaplains aboard the troop ship, Dorchester, in World War II, who gave up their life jackets so others could be saved. "Boy, that took courage."
      Another added, "My sister took shots at the doctor's and didn't even cry."
      They felt each day required some courage especially "to keep on practicing basketball when people say you're no good," "to go against the crowd and not smoke pot," "to work to be a better reader," and "to take the hassle at the bus stop and still come to school."
   b. What are some things you need to do right now in your life that will take courage on your part? When do you want to get started? How will you begin? How can we help you? When can we talk again about your achievement?
      One of our boys was "getting ready" to return to a regular junior high classroom. He thought the transition would take courage on his part. He asked the teachers to help him by making sure he had learned "enough arithmetic and reading to make it." He wanted an opportunity "to visit the school where I'll go" (we arranged a one-day visitation each week for a month's period to help him become acquainted with his homeroom teacher, schedules, lunch room, passing, locker-room procedures, etc.) and to have "My dad take me over some evening to walk through the halls and look around" (the father cooperated with this concern). We talked with the boy each time he returned to Boxelder

from his visits, discussing his feelings, needs, and concerns. He later made a successful transition to the new school.

2. One day we got together old newspapers and scissors and asked the children to look through the newspapers to find acts of courage. This was the beginning of a large mural that stretched across one wall of the dining room. Each day children brought in other clippings to add to the collection. There were many heroic acts reported in the newspapers: fire fighter rescuing people; someone taking an unpopular viewpoint on ecology; a bystander helping people trapped in a car after an accident. On a following day old magazines were used to find other pictures. This led ultimately to each child putting a card on the board with some act of courage he or she had performed. Sometimes an act of courage is nothing more than going to the secretary and asking for a ruler, but for some children that's a very hard thing to do.

STRATEGY NO. 5
because we are human

We asked the children, "What special things can you do just because you're human?" They enumerated several accomplishments: talking with each other, laughing at funny things, coloring in lines, caring for animals, riding a bike, reading books, counting numbers, catching a ball, dancing.

Together we constructed a splashing newsprint collage mural across a twenty foot wall, pasting pictures of people doing human things: kissing, baking cakes, crying, playing, eating spaghetti, working, dancing.

Below the mural, again on newsprint, we drew a long lifeline between birth and twelve years of age. "What were some of the things you learned to do between the ages of birth and five?" we asked. "We learned not to play with matches, not to touch things, not to run away, to go to the bathroom, to walk, talk, and dress ourselves."

The children then placed an X on the line to represent their present age. They were asked, "What have you learned to do from the age of five until now?" "To swim, read, write, play a guitar, multiply, draw pictures, skate, sing, and not run away from home."

We posed another question: "When would you like to leave this school? Place a big L on the age you will be when you would like to leave." Most of the responses were realistic—one, two years—with the exception of one boy who needed the security of belonging in one place. He extended the line beyond the age of twelve to encompass fifteen. "What are some of the things you would expect to learn in the next few years?" "To read better, to finish my lessons, to control my temper, to play with others."

Another individual time line strategy works like this. Obtain string and tack it on one side of the room, running it across to the other side of the room. Each child has his or her own individual string representing birth to the present time. Make a different color tag for each child in the room. A child can have as many tags as wanted. On these tags they paste symbolic pictures, drawings, or sentences about the important events in their lives. Hang these events on the string. The individual events tags spin in the breeze and blow in the wind as the kids walk underneath them. The children can stand on chairs to read what others have written, hung from the different times in their lives.

Still another extension of this strategy is to have the string represent their present lives with a lengthened space for the life they have yet to live. The children can then begin to fantasize some things they want to have happen to them in their lives when they are 20, 30, or 40.

Sam Keen, author, would understand our strategy. He remembers a depressing time during his first grade year when the class practiced penmanship for hours. Sam noticed through the window a warbler building a summer nest. He dreamed of a time when he would be a great ornithologist just as the teacher demanded he finish his work. "Instinct warned me that no serendipitous warbler, no purate fascination could provide an excuse for the neglect of my serious educational duties . . . it was tacitly assumed that education had no responsibility for helping me come to terms with the particular, the concrete, the idiosyncratic, the biographical, and the sensuous facts which formed the substance of my private existence. I learned little about the organization, appreciation, management and care of that unique piece of human real estate which bears the legal name Sam Keen."[6] Thanks, Sam, for sharing this wonder and wisdom.

STRATEGY NO. 6 ——————————————————
a quiet spot

Leonardo da Vinci said, "Every now and then go away, have a little relaxation, for when you come back to your work your judgement will be surer, since to remain constantly at work will cause you to lose power of judgement. Go some distance away, because then the work appears smaller, and more of it can be taken in at a glance, and a lack of harmony or proportion is more readily seen."

"Every now and then go away," replenish your energy, then come

[6]Keen, Sam, *To A Dancing God*, Harper and Row, New York, 1970, pp. 39–40.

back stronger! We sometimes help children find relaxing memories of places and things by closing their eyes and remembering:

> the smell of freshly baked cookies,
> the feel of warm sunshine,
> the quiet rustling of leaves,
> a soft, warm bed,
> cool rain on a hot summer's day,
> being with someone you love,
> a bird soaring high in the blue sky,
> a meadow of flowers,
> your favorite piece of music,
> puffy white clouds,
> a beautiful sunset,
> a place where you like to be alone,
> a warm hug,
> the sound of a stream,
> doing something for someone,
> a good laugh,
> the quiet of night,
> a bird singing.

As the children relax their minds, their bodies also relax. As the last relaxing suggestion, we tell them to count silently from 4 backwards to 1 and when they open their eyes they will feel relaxed and refreshed.

STRATEGY NO. 7 ——————————————————————
a place for me[7]

One of the principle tenets of Gestalt psychology is *awareness*—a tuning in on internal awareness of mind and especially body sensations as to how people and situations affect our emotions. There are people who make us feel blah, bored, fatigued, or angry. These deep internal feelings alert us to the toxic people in our lives. Situations are also toxic, for instance room design or color can promote feelings of dis-ease, tension, even hyperactivity.

We ask our children to close their eyes and imagine their rooms at home. What do they remember, what do they see, how do they feel in their room? Are there aspects of the room they don't like, such as bright lights, crowded conditions, clutter? What effects do their rooms have on them? Is it possible to change their room arrangement? How could they do this to make their rooms more comfortable, more pleasant? We discuss these possibilities with each child in the group. As one child tells about his or her room, the others make constructive suggestions for improving it.

Finally we ask the children to draw their rooms and make any necessary changes that would make the living arrangements more ideal. Questions help the process of planning:

What things do you want in your room?

What colors are best for you?

Will other people share your room? If so, can you arrange for some privacy if that is important to you?

Are there places for studying, sleeping, and playing in your room?

In this strategy we work with children to discover what is important to them and how they can include these factors in a room of their own. As a followup activity we invite parents to see the drawings of the rooms and ask for their help and suggestions in bringing about the type of room their child wishes to live in.

One of the boys drew the plan on the following page of how he would like his room to be. At the time he felt "ripped off" because many of the things that had made his room "a special place" had been removed.

[7]The idea for this strategy was suggested by Nancy Diedrich, an elementary counselor in the Poudre R-1 schools.

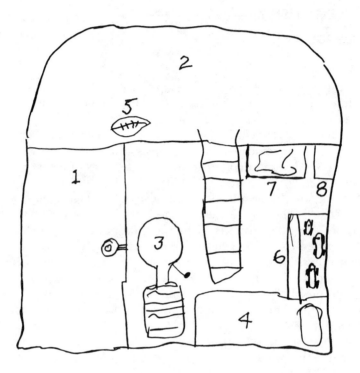

1. "This is the door to my room."
2. "This is the attic where I used to play. I kept all my toys up there but they (mother-father) boarded it up and took away the ladder so I can't go up there anymore. But I still do and they don't know it!"
3. "I use to have a lamp but my sis ripped it off. I wish I had that back."
4. "That's my bed and pillow."
5. "I keep the football upstairs in the attic."
6. "That's my shelf with my models. I made car models but I don't have them anymore 'cause they caused a mess."
7. "I did have a poster there but my sis got that in her room, too."
8. "I wish I had my window back but I broke it with my basketball and it's all boarded up."

FOUR

love
strategies

Abe Maslow once lamented in an introduction to Pitrim Sorokin's book, *The Power of Love*, that psychologists were so seemingly unconcerned about love and knew so little about it that the word, *love*, was seldom indexed in any psychological book. Maslow, himself, knew that, "The need for love characterizes every human being that was ever born,"[1] and he wrote extensively about this need and the capacity to love. To him need and capacity were synonymous. He wrote, "Not only is it fun to use our capacities but it is necessary for growth."[2] He felt that love, when unused as a skill or capacity, would become the center of disease and thus diminish the person as a human being. So he sought to teach others about the therapeutic, redeeming qualities of love. He felt the full development of a human being was not possible unless that person was capable of receiving and giving love.

Many children suffer from "love-hunger," a deficiency disease that ". . . if caught early enough, replacement therapy can cure"[3]—that is, the pathological deficiency can be made up. We realize all children's needs to receive as well as to give love so we have included seven strategies that focus on love:

1. Things I Love (an inventory of love objects and how love is given)
2. A Man Named Zorba (to help children rediscover their individual fascination and love with nature and other human beings)
3. The Wish Book—Love Received (another way of loving through validation)
4. Love Shared (an opportunity to experience the joy of love through giving)
5. My Cookie Person (reflections and memories of closeness and love)
6. Prerequisites to Love (providing for safety needs so that love can emerge)
7. Becoming Aware of Love (a week of strategies to explore the ways and power of love)

Maslow saw love need as a deficit need. "It is a hole which has to be filled, an emptiness into which love is poured. If this healing necessity is not available, severe pathology results; if it is available at the right time, in the right quantities and with proper style, then pathology is averted."[4]

[1]Maslow, Abraham H., *Toward a Psychology of Being*, Van Nostrand Reinhold, New York, 1968, p. 191.
[2]Ibid, p. 201.
[3]Ibid, p. 42.
[4]Maslow, *Toward a Psychology of Being*, p. 41.

Our children are all love-hungry. Without exception this is true. We hope to provide some love experiences in their lives trusting that, "If the pathology is not too severe and if it is caught early enough, replacement therapy can cure."[5]

STRATEGY NO. 1
things I love

We agree with Chardin, who thought that one day, after gaining control over the elements of wind, sea, and gravity, people would learn of the energy contained in love. This impact, he thought, would be as important as the discovery of fire. Humans have pretty well "mastered" the elements of the world in this twentieth century. For us, now, with this small group of children, the time is ripe for learning to love in simple ways.

Tom T. Hall is a young man who writes country music and tells down-to-earth stories. One of his songs, "I Love" from his album "For The People In The Last Hard Town" (Mercury Records), won our hearts and the hearts of the children. We play his record as an introduction to this strategy. Tom's lyrics tell about some of the simple things in life he has found to be loveable:

> baby ducks,
> country streams,
> birds, squirrels,
> kisses and smiles.

After the record we asked the children to form into small groups and draw something they have loved. These objects of love could include people or things. (We provided each child with *one* colored crayon so that drawings could be completed in a shorter time without laboring over color selection, detailing, etc. The exercise was intended to provoke an idea or value, not a work of art.)

When the drawings were completed the children returned to the large group to share their pictures. They were asked to explain *what* they loved and *how* they gave their love in that instance. After each child talked, the teacher summarized how love was shown in a particular way by that child and enumerated all the "ways of love" on a large sheet of

[5]Maslow, *Toward a Psychology of Being*, p. 42.

newsprint. As the examples below show, this strategy helps children extend their love to many living things. Perhaps in time their love will grow, like Albert Schweitzer's, to include every living thing in a deep reverence for life.

"I love birds and flowers. I would never shoot a bird or pick a flower." (The teacher wrote, *"Caring* is a way of loving.")

"I love flowers. I talk to them. I water them and give them sunshine." ("Being with, and talking to are other ways of loving.")

"I love ducks. I made mine a pen. I feed them and give them water." ("Protecting is a way of loving.")

"I love my Mom. I buy presents for her whenever I can." ("Giving gifts shows love.")

"I love my dog. I never hit him or put a leash on him. I take him for walks. I hug him." ("Hugs are a great way to show love as well as giving people and animals the freedom they need to grow.")

"I love the mountains. I share them with other people by walking with them along the mountain trails." ("Sharing the things we love is loving.")

"I love holidays and weekends. I try not to argue with my family at these times." ("Consideration of other people's feelings is a way of loving.")

"I love the mountains and nature, the trees, the sky. I don't cause fires." ("Being considerate and sensitive.")

"I love people. I visit them and say, 'hi.' I smile at them and give them a hand if they need it." ("Smiling, helping, and being friendly are beautiful ways to say 'I love you.' ")

Sigmund Freud once defined a healthy person as one who:

1. Was able to love someone.
2. Was able to be loved by someone.
3. Was able to find work he or she considered to be necessary and important to do.

In this activity there is no gap between LOVE + WORK or CREED + DEED. The children acted in ways consistent with their beliefs, thoughtful conceptualization carried through in concrete action. This really is what the valuing process is all about: Choosing—Prizing —Acting![6]

---

[6]Raths, Louis, *et al.*, *Values and Teaching;* Charles E. Merrill, Columbus, Ohio, 1966. Simon, Sidney *et al.*, *Values Clarification, A Handbook of Practical Strategies for Teachers and Students,* Hart, New York, 1972.

STRATEGY NO. 2
a man named Zorba

One crisp autumn afternoon we thought it might be rewarding to help the children rediscover their individual fascination with nature and with other human beings. We wondered what activities might provide them with opportunities to look and really see objects and people and to regain their sense of wonder. We wanted them to be like Zorba the Greek, to delight in themselves, in nature, and in others. Since Zorba, who discovered the secret of living with zest and joy, who was continually amazed at what he saw whether it be a child, a star, a tree, or a glass of cold water, might be someone children would be interested in hearing about, we told them this story:

Everyday the world was new to Zorba. His eyes looked deep into the nature of things and understood. Once he was fascinated and amazed as he drank a glass of cold wine. He remembered back to where wine had its beginning, to the small sour green grapes that became sweet and juicy as they ripened in the warm sun. He thought about how they were then crushed to make wine and the wine stored in casks finally to be drunk at a time of celebration where people danced and sang. It was always a mystery to Zorba how grapes could be changed to wine; wine changed to energy and happiness, to dancing and singing.

Zorba lived his life with all of his five senses. He breathed in the smell of the sea and forest. He listened to birds singing. He watched the leaves turn in autumn. He loved the taste of vegetable soup and homemade bread. He was intrigued with the softness of a rose petal. He kept his body in good shape too because he loved to run, to wrestle, swim, ride horses, and work hard. He found joy in everything he did.

We then told the children we wanted them to experience life as Zorba did, to really look and see things that, perhaps, they pass over every day because the things seem common when really they are quite beautiful if we but pause to really look and question.

The group was asked to be very quiet as we went outdoors for a nature walk. (If your school is in an urban area have the children bring fruit, leaves, shells, rocks, etc. the day before your group meets.) As they silently walked, they were to find one object such as a rock or a leaf that caused them to wonder. Each discovery was to be brought back to the group for sharing.

When the students returned they were instructed to begin a sentence with,

"I see_____."

They were not especially romantic about their nature collections nor did they show deep insights into nature's secrets, but they did see beyond just rocks, leaves, and branches. It is our continued hope that someday great gobs of insight and depth will develop in our children. These beginnings are the start of that great hope:

> A rock: "I see a tiny, shiny spot of glitter in this smooth rock."
>
> A leaf: "I see pretty colors, brown, yellow and orange."
>
> A split branch: "I see where the water came up the branch from the roots; it's brown there."

(A good book to read to children is Rachel Carson's *The Sense Of Wonder*, Harper and Row, New York, 1956. Her book is illustrated with beautiful nature photography for children.)

As a last experience in seeing we asked each child in turn to sit in a "spotlight chair." The other children then tried to look at that child as if for the first time or as if they saw something in the focus child they had never seen before. It was a time for looking with deeper understanding than ever before. Each child began a sentence with:

> "I see_____."

These are sample statements from the group:

> To a boy: "I see a good friend."
>
> To another boy: "I see a person who is really trying to grow up and not be silly anymore."
>
> To a girl: "I see a girl who is fun to play with."
>
> To another girl: "I see a girl who thinks for herself."
>
> To a boy: "I see a happy boy."
>
> To a girl: "I see someone who shares things (with others)."

Perhaps love begins with objects like rocks and trees and then gradually grows until it is able to encompass humankind. But with everything there must be a simple beginning. You can help your children begin the journey. The Zorba way.

STRATEGY NO. 3 ⎯⎯⎯⎯⎯⎯⎯⎯⎯⎯⎯⎯⎯
the wish book—love received

We have begun a tradition at our school to continue with expressions of love and validation for the therapeutic effects they have both on the person receiving as well as the one giving. Each time someone new is taken into our group, we give this person a "Wish Book."[7] The children are each given a sheet of construction paper to draw or paste pictures of things they wish for the new student. Before the pages are stapled together to form a booklet of good wishes, each child brings his or her page and gives it to the new child, interpreting wishes. These are moments of warm intimacy as the children verbalize their wishes:

> "I wish for you a snowmobile and mountains, houses, barns, and blue skies." (A collage)

> "I wish for you ice-cream cones, books to read, friends to play with, and chocolate cake." (A drawing)

> "I wish for you a room full of butterflies." (A drawing)

At these moments we glimpse some of the warmth, romance, and fantastic possibilities of these children who, at other times, seem almost insensitive to the needs of others. We see also the feeling of being worthy of love, the self-acceptance that gives the new child an opportunity to grow from the very first day at the new school.

An interesting follow-through strategy is to schedule a series of important interviews over a two-week period with the new child and the other children. In these interviews the children really begin to know the new person. They wish some new things based partially on their interviews and their experiences over the two weeks the new child has been in school with them.

STRATEGY NO. 4 ⎯⎯⎯⎯⎯⎯⎯⎯⎯⎯⎯⎯⎯
love shared

Most of our children suffer from love hunger, a deficiency that causes them to seek love from others selfishly. They increasingly tend to use

---

[7]This idea was given to us by Dennis Miller, Jr. High Counselor for the Poudre R-1 Schools, Ft. Collins, Colorado.

people in their demand for more and more love. Seldom are they able to give love, which denies them the intrinsic joy of sharing love.

We have developed two strategies that can be experienced at any time but which are probably most appropriate during Thanksgiving, Chanukah, and Christmas.

At Christmas (Chanukah) we ask the children what personal gift of themselves, their time, or their energy could they give their parents in the form of a gift certificate. We divided into small subgroups to consider all the possibilities. The final example selections were gift certificates redeemable for specific services:

{ For Dad: a basement cleanup during the vacation.
{ For Mom: washing all the dishes from the big holiday dinner.

{ For Dad: cleaning out the garage.
{ For Mom: one free dusting of the house plants and one free dishwashing.

{ For Dad: help him take down the decorations.
{ For Mom: help her make all the beds.

For Mom: take out the garbage two days (no father in the house).

{ For Dad: stay out of your way when you're doing something.
{ For Mom: clean my room and feed the fish.

For Mom: one free egg sandwich made by me and one free dishwashing (no father in the house).

For Mom: clean up the house on Christmas Day (no father in the house).

We took sheets of typing paper, folded them once, and on the inside sheet the children wrote the value exchange of each certificate. The outside cover was decorated individually by each child. In order to insure delivery each certificate was sent by U.S. mail.

The week before Thanksgiving we asked the children to list all of the things they had taken from their world the past week. We wrote the long list on newsprint. We then asked what, in turn, had they given back to their world. Again a list was made to show the balance/imbalance between giving/taking. There was a definite imbalance in our group in the direction of "taking."

Because our teachers give so much of their energy and consideration to children, we decided to validate their efforts especially at Thanksgiving. We again asked the children to make a list of things teachers had given them versus things they had given teachers during the past week:

1. What We Gave Teachers (other than a "bad time")
   a. Helped in the kitchen.
   b. Watched and helped with the other kids.

     c. Brought books and supplies to school.
     d. Went right to work without a hassle.
     e. Cooperated with a substitute teacher.
2. What Teachers Gave Us
     a. Helped me with exercises.
     b. Talked with me.
     c. Helped with reading and math.
     d. Helped me build a fort.
     e. Played with me at recess.
     f. Let me cook.
     g. Gave us juice and cookies.
     h. Helped me when I hurt.
     i. Let me tape record my voice.
     j. Let me visit his Love-Care Group.
     k. Sat with me at lunch.

This was simply an exercise in awareness. Nothing more was said after the lists were compiled. Sometimes we, like the Gestalt psychologists, feel awareness is enough because it can eventually lead to behavioral change. In reality, changed behavior is what we are really after.

STRATEGY NO. 5 ——————————————————
my cookie person

In this simple yet deeply moving strategy, we ask the children to each find a place where they can sit alone and think back over the years to a person who loved them very much—"a cookie person." We call these loving people "cookie persons" because perhaps this was their way of expressing their love:

    by giving a cookie—

    a hug

    or a word of encouragement

Between long pauses, we ask our children to remember their cookie person as if it were yesterday and they had met again. What was their particular person like? How did that person care for them? What did the person do? How did they feel when they were with their cookie person? What about them as children made the cookie person love them?

    Usually the children smile as they reflect upon these happy memories and we have been gratified to learn that every child we have worked with has had a loving person, somewhere, in his or her life. If, by chance, someday we meet a lonely child who has not known that kind of love, one of us would quickly assume the loving responsibility of being a "cookie person."

After the children share their cookie person, we tell them this is an important story for them to remember and retell often because this person, perhaps as much as any person they will ever meet, taught them their first lesson in loving, caring, and giving.

We always end each "cookie person strategy" by asking the children who they are a cookie person to: who looks to them for love? Because we feel, too, that ". . . in the sense in which man can ever be said to be at home in the world, he is at home not through dominating, or explaining, or appreciating, but through caring and being cared for."[8]

Responses from Our Children:

"My cookie person is Grandma Schroeder. She's 80 years old and came from Germany. She gives me spice cookies and onions from her garden. She let's me play her music box. She says when she dies she's going to give it to me. She makes me feel good but I'll be sad if she dies." (Dean, age 10)

"I'm a cookie person to my mom. I obey her and don't give her a hard time." (Bob, age 9)

"My junior league football coach is my cookie guy. He just keeps me going. When I get hurt he'd say, 'It's okay. Sit down and take it easy for awhile.' He always compliments me on the good plays and tells me it is okay when I miss a pass. I want to do my best for him . . . want to do it right. He makes me feel wanted and happy. I work hard. I won't quit. I think that's why he likes me. I'm a cookie person to the other guys on the team. I give them compliments and help them when they're hurt." (Mark, age 11)

STRATEGY NO. 6

prerequisites to love

Maslow once described man as "perceptually wanting." He wrote that the basic "wants" or needs are, in ascending order: food, safety, love, esteem, and for some, self actualization.[9] He felt that as one need was satisfied another emerged in what he viewed as a hierarchy of needs. We have used Maslow's theory with our children in a very practical way.

[8]Mayeroff, Milton, *On Caring*, Perennial Library, Harper and Row, New York, 1971, p. 2.
[9]Wilson, Colin, *New Pathways in Psychology*, New American Library, New York, 1972, pp. 148–49.

Children who are hungry find it difficult to conceive of any other need except food. Their empty stomachs preclude learning. Therefore, we make sure our children have had their breakfast each morning, and if they haven't, we feed them toast and milk or cereal. As do most schools, at noon we provide a nourishing meal. Their basic physiological need for food is thus satisfied.

When the physiological needs are satisfied, the "safety" needs emerge. These include freedom from pain or fear and the need for a regular routine to make the world a somewhat predictable place to live. For many of our children the world around them has been rather fearful and threatening. They have known sickness, failure, divorce, high mobility, poverty, and all sorts of uncomfortable conditions. Unable to make many successful predictions, they have experienced chronic states of anxiety, stress, and turmoil.

We have felt that our teachers and the children themselves hold the potential for being the main sources of safety and nurturance. We wanted to provide a safe environment, a regular schedule, and a predictable day so that the children would feel more free to learn. One way to promote safety is through reasonable, enforceable rules.

In a group session, early in the year, we ask children to suggest a few rules they thought would be necessary in making school a good, safe place to be. These suggestions are usually expressed in "don'ts": "don't hit other people," "don't cuss or use bad words," "don't mess up the toilets," etc. From these ideas we formulated three simple rules regarding people and things:

1. "None of us has the right to hurt another person." We then discuss how people are hurt: by physical abuse, by words, by being ignored, etc.
2. "None of us has the right to turn our hurt against ourselves." We ask how we do this: by pouting and withdrawing, by actual physical harm, by screaming till our throats hurt, etc.
3. "None of us has the right to destroy property." The children then talk about some of the destructiveness they have experienced—smashing toys, writing on walls, throwing food, etc.

Helpful suggestions on how to enforce rules come from Judith and Donald Smith, who think that in most instances asking a child for a "restatement of the rule" is sufficient. "Whenever a child breaks the rule, ask him (unemotionally), 'What's the rule?' . . . We have used this method with classes of normal and problem children . . . our experience indicates that it is more effective and easier to use than any system of punishments and penalties."

From our experience with troubled children, we have found the above approach quite successful. Here are three examples:

1. John "punches out" Larry and takes over the swing. The conversation goes something like this:

Teacher: "What's the rule, John?"

John: "Yeah, I know, you ain't supposed to hurt someone."

Teacher: "OK, I expect you not to."

John: "All right, take the swing, Larry."

(Sometimes it is just that simple. Try it and see!)

2. Don refuses to celebrate one of the children's birthdays by eating cake and ice cream. Instead he crumples in a corner feeling very much alienated.

Teacher: "What's a rule we made, Don?"

Don: "I don't know."

Teacher: "Remember, three rules for the school. . . . What are you doing?"

Don: "Nothing."

Teacher: "Not really breaking any rule, huh?"

Don: "No."

Teacher: "I think you're breaking the one about hurting yourself. I hate to see you do that. Come on and join us."

If Don comes back to the group nothing more is said. If he does not he suffers the natural consequences of his behavior. He misses the celebration.

3. Betty smashes the roof of the doll house in anger.

Teacher: "What's the rule, Betty?"

Betty: "Don't destroy property."

At this point the teacher probably asks, "What can you do now?" In this way Betty faces the reality of her behavior and is asked to be responsible for that behavior. The teacher helps her consider alternatives, for example, repair the roof, buy a new doll house, do nothing at all, ask someone else to fix it, destroy the remainder of the doll house.

The children know we together accepted rules for their own, as well as our own protection. They are assured daily that we care for them, and they understand we will be consistent in teaching them to be responsible. Because of this, they usually respond with a reasonable plan of action. If, in a rare instance, they choose to be irresponsible, to test our or their own power, we would insist that the rules we collectively agreed to at the beginning of the year be considered a binding contract. We, as their teachers, would choose one of the alternatives and ask them to honor our decision or suffer further consequences which might be (in the third case) one of the following:

1. Rejection by the other children for not obeying rules that others are expected to obey, and further rejection because the doll house is no longer an enjoyable toy.
2. Calling the parents, asking them to pay for the damaged doll house.
3. Making all of the school toys "off limits" to Betty until the damage is repaired, etc.

Some children will test limits and they will manipulate situations to determine if teachers are really consistent. After a time this behavior diminishes and they are assured, "This place is safe! I can count on these teachers. I can learn to be responsible here." Thus they are ready to move toward the next level, satisfying the need for love.

Maslow was always interested in how people evaded growth— what held them up— what blocked them. As a partial, tentative answer he talked and wrote about the "Jonah Complex." "So often we run away from the responsibilities dictated (or rather suggested) by nature, by fate, even sometimes by accident, just as Jonah tried–in vain–to run away from his fate."[10] There is a fear of growing, a fear of progressing from what we know into the unknown, a fear even of growing out of our neurosis into normality. Children, as well as adults, need consistent support as they are invited to eschew irresponsible behavior and grow toward maturity. Responsibility cannot be given; it must be learned by being immersed in living. Life and experience offer the best textbook, the best classroom for learning. Dr. William Glasser states, "An agreement to see the patient and help him solve his problems is basic to beginning therapy . . . the promise is made in some form . . . 'I will see you until you can become better able to fulfill your needs.' "[11]

STRATEGY NO. 7
becoming aware of love

With the assurances of a safe, consistent environment, children may grow toward loving, responsible behavior, overcoming outmoded, static, even destructive ways of being. Oliver Wendell Holmes wrote, "Man's mind stretched to a new idea never goes back to its original dimensions." In this strategy we stretch children's hearts and minds to encompass love.

[10]Maslow, Abraham H., *The Farther Reaches of Human Nature*, Viking Press, New York, 1971, p. 35.
[11]Glasser, William, *Reality Therapy*, Harper and Row, New York, 1965, p. 36.

We begin by scheduling each day of one week for the consideration of love as it affects each of our lives.

Monday: The children and teachers find a secluded spot where they can meditate and remember how and when love came to them. They are asked to recall: By whom and how have I been loved in the past? How has love come to me in the week just passed? A discussion follows with each child giving one or two instances of love and its effect on his or her life.

Tuesday: Children and teachers take time to reflect for a few moments on another two questions: How have I given love in the past? How have I shown love this past week? As before, children and teachers select one or two acts of personal love they would be willing to share in a group. As an assignment for Wednesday everyone is asked to bring in newspapers for the group discussion. No further elaboration is made except to say that newspapers from any day in the past week are fine to bring.

Wednesday: Because some of our children have difficulty reading, we assign small groups of children to a teacher and together they quickly read through three newspapers. They clip each report of love and each report of violence and hatred. Back in the large group these reports are read and the headlines printed on a sheet of newsprint to see the balance between love and hate in the world. Two advanced assignments are given for Thursday and Friday at this time. For Thursday each child and teacher is asked to search for a poem or story about love. For Friday each is asked to bring in a record or a song about love.

Thursday: Time is scheduled throughout the day (between study time, recess, lunch, etc.) to gather together for short periods of reading poems and stories of love.

Friday: The same format as Thursday is followed with time provided to hear records and songs of love.

At the end of this week's sessions the children are asked to write "I learned," "I wish," and "I wonder" statements about love. These are made into posters using original drawings or illustrations from magazines and hang all over the school.

Pitrim Sorokin has listed the "psychological aspects of love"[12] as follows:

---

[12]Sorokin, Pitrim, *The Ways and Power of Love*, Henry Regnery, Chicago, 1967, pp. 11–12.

" . . . love is the experience that annuls our individual loneliness . . . love is literally a life-giving force . . . love beautifies our life . . . love experience means freedom at its loftiest . . . love is a feeling of fearlessness and power . . . the love experience is equivalent to the highest peace of mind and happiness."

Through the writings of Erich Fromm we learned that love is an art. This awareness of what love is constitutes the first step in the process of learning to be a loving person. The second step is to practice love. Taken together these seven love strategies can provide children with opportunities to discover the qualities of love and ways to express and practice the art.

FIVE

values

brainstorming life's values
boxes–boxes–boxes
change
what'ja learn today?
Charlie from outer space
a penny for your thoughts
future worlds

Early in his writing Louis Raths alluded to "value disturbances" in children and suggested that there ". . . is strong support for the notion that (a lack of) values must be added to the possible explanations of children's behavior problems."[1] Children who were unclear or confused about their own values appeared to be more "apathetic, flighty, uncertain or inconsistent, drifters, overconformers, overdissenters, or role players." Rath began to ask, "Could it be . . . that the pace and complexity of modern life has so exacerbated the problem of deciding what is good and what is right and what is worthy and what is desirable that large numbers of children are finding it increasingly bewildering, even overwhelming, to decide what is worth valuing, what is worth one's time and energy?"[2] Raths set about developing a process, a methodology, to help people clarify their own values and thereby give their own lives more purpose, enthusiasm, and pride.

Maslow also was concerned with human values and their effect on behavior: "The state of being without a system of values is psychopathogenic, we are learning. The human being needs a framework of values, a philosophy of life . . . in about the same sense that he needs sunlight, calcium, or love . . . we need a validated, usable system of human values that we can believe in and devote ourselves to. . . ."[3] "It is necessary, in order for children to grow well, that adults have enough trust in them and in the natural processes of growth . . . to let them grow and help them in a taoistic rather than an authoritarian way."[4]

Rogers said, "Experience for me is the highest authority. The touchstone of validity is my own experience. . . . My experience is not authoritative because it is infallible. It is the basis of authority because it can be checked in new primary ways. In this way its frequent error or fallibility is always open to correction."[5]

Throughout our book we have attempted to combine these men's philosophies to order to: (1) follow a process of values clarification that helps children consider alternatives; (2) be Taoistic in our approach; (3)

---

[1]Raths, Louis E., Harmin, Merrill, and Simon, Sidney, *Values and Teaching, Working With Values in the Classroom*, Chas. E. Merrill, Columbus, Ohio, 1966, p. 4.
[2]Ibid, p. 7.
[3]Maslow, Abraham H., *Toward a Psychology of Being*, Van Nostrand Reinhold, New York, 1968, p. 206.
[4]*Perceiving, Behaving, Becoming*, Assoc. for Supervision & Curriculum Development, National Education Association, Washington 6, D.C., 1962, p. 198.
[5]Rogers, Carl R., *On Becoming a Person*, Houghton Mifflin, Boston, 1961, pp. 23 and 24.

value the person's own experience in realizing that the locus of valuing must come from within the person.

Seven of our strategies consider values:

1. Brainstorming Life's Values (thoughtful consideration of what things have priority in life)
2. Boxes—Boxes—Boxes (a feeling-thinking approach to values)
3. Change (acting upon beliefs and values)
4. What'ja Learn Today (being open to experience)
5. Charlie from Outer Space (affirmation of belief)
6. A Penny for Your Thoughts (an exercise in discovering cultural values)
7. Future Worlds (creating and improvising a world of the future)

STRATEGY NO. 1 ——————————————————————————
brainstorming life's values

The highest of life's values are often expressed in groups of threes:

1. Life
2. Liberty
3. The pursuit of happiness   (Thomas Jefferson, statesman)

1. Women
2. Fruit
3. Ideas   (Nikos Kazantzakis, novelist)

1. Children
2. Old dogs
3. Watermelon wine   (Tom T. Hall, composer)

It is a difficult task to sift, refine, and condense life's essentials into groups of three. The process requires reflection, free choice, alternatives, prizing, affirming, and, in the case of the above three philosophies, acting. Each one of these men acted upon what he believed and made his values a part of the pattern of his living.

We brainstormed with children one day those things they felt were most important. We began with "What are the most important things to you?" There was a barrage of answers: "ducks, busses, books, grades, school, pets, birds, fun, math, people, kids." On a large sheet of newsprint we made drawings of all these valuable, important things in life. Then we discussed the value of each child's choice and why he had chosen his particular thing. Ducks were important because "they ate insects," busses because they "carried kids to school," kids because "we just are." We then asked for a vote to decide the top three. The results were:

1. Kids are most important.
2. People are important.
3. Pets are important.

In descending order came school, busses, birds, ducks, and finally math.

On another day we followed the same brainstorming–discussing –setting priorities pattern using "parents" as the subject for investigation. We asked, "What things do parents consider important?" The children ordered their responses as follows:

1. The family is most important.
2. Pets are important.
3. Money is important.
4. T.V. is important.

A further activity includes having the children take this list of priorities home and discuss the family's priorities at the dinner table to see how different families would actually vote. Many other excellent family strategies are developed in a section entitled "Values in the Family" from the book, *Readings in Value Clarification,* by Sidney Simon and Howard Kirschenbaum, Winston Press, Minneapolis, 1973. Also see our section on *Parent Involvement* and our Appendix.

STRATEGY NO. 2
boxes—boxes—boxes

E. E. Cummings once wrote about the endless, tough battle each one of us fights to be "nobody-but-yourself." The world, he thought, fights stubbornly to make us a conglomeration, an amalgamation of other people's thoughts and values. This is especially true of childhood when many adults—teachers, preachers, parents, salespeople—impose rather than explore values with the younger-than-themselves.

Children live in a confusing sometimes bewildering world of "shoulds," "oughts," and "nevers" out of which they must bring some order for themselves—some way of realistically coping with life's many problems—some way of making decisions—some way of believing for oneself, or trusting one's own experience. This strategy offers students the opportunity to discover values for themselves through the complete process of *choosing—prizing—acting*, a process that inherently values both thinking and feeling experiences. The *boxes—boxes—boxes* strategy allows many children to express how they feel, what they believe, how they act in certain instances—a process of sharing values.

We have constructed several brightly colored boxes. Each box contains questions on areas where most children experience some confusion and conflict in values:

Family
School
Myself
Money—Possessions
Friends

Other boxes could include questions about work, religion, love—on any subject about life that touches a concern—a choice of childhood. We have listed the *friends* with sample questions as an example:

Friends Questions Box

1. What is the most fun you have ever had with a friend?
2. Can you remember receiving a gift from a friend? What was it?
3. Can you remember giving a gift to a friend? What was it?
4. What is the longest time you have ever had one friend? What were some of the things you did together during that time?
5. How do you feel most of the time when you are with your friend? Why do you feel this way?
6. (Boy) Do you ever enjoy playing with girls?
7. (Girl) Do you ever enjoy playing with boys?
8. What hobbies does your friend have? Are you interested in the same things?
9. What is a new thing you and your friend have learned to do?
10. Do you wish you were more popular? What could you do or be that would help people like you more?
11. How many good friends do you have? How many do you think you need?
12. If you had two hours to spend with your friend, what would you like to do?
13. Are you a loner? Why?
14. How do you handle a person who picks on you?
15. What are some of the things you like about your best friend?
16. What things do you like to do when you are with a friend?

17. How does your friend help you? How do you help your friend?
18. What do your friends like about you?
19. Have you ever fought with your friend? About what? How did you make up?
20. Are your friends better than you? If so, in what ways are they better?
21. Are you better than your friends? If so, how are you better?
22. Are your friends older than you or younger? Why is this?

We ask the children to choose (by voting) for their box of interest for the day.

Children are than asked to volunteer to reach in the box and pull out one question. The teacher helps them read the question and they answer as best they can from their experience. Other children can share by reacting and entering the discussion after each child talks. No put-down statements are allowed from the group. This session emphasizes respect and acceptance of another person's point of view.

Carl Rogers wrote, "I have found it highly rewarding when I can accept another person . . . acceptance does not come easy. . . . I believe that it is an increasingly common pattern in our culture for each of us to believe, every other person must feel and think and believe the same as I do . . . yet . . . the right of each individual to utilize his experience in his own way and to discover his own meaning in it, this is one of the most priceless potentialities of life."[6]

STRATEGY NO. 3

change

"As a man thinks in his heart so is he," taught Jesus.

"What a man does reveals his values," say the existentialists.

"Behind each value is a feeling," write modern psychologists.

Indeed the process of valuing includes thinking, feeling, and acting, no one excluding the others. In this strategy we ask children how they feel, what they think, and how they can take action to bring about change.

We gave each child a large sheet of paper with spaces for school, home, city, county, state, nation, world, and me.

Then we asked each child to spend ten minutes alone and write in the changes he or she would like to see in any of the above areas (teachers helped those who could not write). School—Home—Me—and

---

[6]Rogers, *On Becoming a Person*, pp. 20–21.

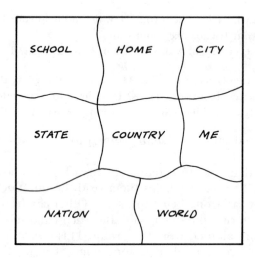

World were the most productive areas for us, but we have included the others as possible stimulus for your particular group.

In their *homes* children would like to change:

"My brothers' always picking on me."

"My father (now divorced) seeing me more often on weekends."

"A room of my own where I can keep my own things."

School changes:

"More playground equipment."

"More time in wood work."

"Chips for rewards."

Me changes:

"So I don't get mad so easy."

"Be a better reader."

"Talk more in our group."

World changes:

"Don't kill the whales in the ocean."

"Increase speed limits."

"Stop pollution."

We requested that children each choose one area of change they were most interested in and tell the group about it. The group then helped the individual consider alternative ways of action for bringing about change. Each child was then asked to choose a plan of action and to the best of his or her ability carry it through. The results were to be reported in two weeks.

A girl who wanted her father to visit her more often dictated the following letter to her dad:

> Dear Dad,
>
> I would like to see you more often because I miss you very much. If you have the time I would like to see you once a week. Would you please answer me in a letter?
>
> Love,
> Susie

We "cleared" the letter first with Susie's mother and then sent it by mail. Other children talked with their parents and teachers about changes they would like to see. Their efforts were met with both success and failure as often happens in a real world that, at times, resists change.

Followup activities included writing letters or calling by phone people who had brought about positive change. These people need validation too!

Earl C. Kelley once wrote of the fully functioning person as one who "... sees himself as part of a world in movement—in process of becoming. ... He will not search for a firm foundation on which he can stand for the rest of his life. He will realize that the only thing he knows for sure about the future is that tomorrow will be different from today and that he can anticipate this difference with hopeful expectation."[7]

STRATEGY NO. 4 ————————————————
what'ja learn today?

Leo Buscaglia in his warm, captivating book about love reminisces about his Italian family: their traditions, beliefs and values. They loved, among other things, spaghetti, veal, garlic, singing, and new ideas. New ideas were especially important to Leo's "papa" who, after supper, smoked his little black cigar, leaned back in his chair and asked, "What did you learn new today?" He expected his children to grow in the acquisition of

[7]*Perceiving, Behaving, Becoming,* Assoc. for Supervision and Curriculum Development, Washington, D.C., 1962, p. 19.

knowledge each day they lived. Leo and his sister always managed an answer to their papa's question even if they had to quickly look up a fact or two in the encyclopedia before supper. Their father was always excited and pleased with their response, nothing seemed insignificant to him.[8]

We told our children about this Italian gentleman and how he valued new ideas. We then said we would provide them with three opportunities to learn new things. The activities included listening to a record, hearing a short story, and either drawing a picture or discussing a topic of interest.

We first played two selections from John Denver's album, *Back Home Again* (RCA Records), "It's Up To You" and "Cool an' Green and Shady." (You may wish to choose your own record to stimulate ideas.) We had no preconceived notion as to what particular thoughts these songs would motivate. They were simply easy-to-listen-to and enjoyable, a now experience if nothing more.

Then we read a book, "What If Everybody Did?" by JoAnn Stover (David McKay Company, New York, 1960). This little book is a delight in considering imaginative, fantastic consequences of children's actions. As with the record, other favorite books may be substituted for your particular group of children.

After these listening experiences we asked the group to choose one of three topics and pair off with one other person to:

1. Draw a picture together about anything they choose.
2. Take turns discussing the high point and low point of their past week. Each child talked uninterrupted for three minutes while his or her partner listened. After three minutes their roles changed.
3. Discuss one change they would like to make in the way their school was run.

After six minutes we asked all the children to return to the circle and share one new idea from any of the three activities. Among their "I learned" statements were:

"I learned to listen."

"I learned I'm not dumb."

"I learned we can change things."

"I learned I can talk in a group."

One group of two who had discussed changing the school thought

[8]Buscaglia, Leo F., *Love*, Chas. B. Slack, Thorofare, New Jersey, 1972, p. 17.

posters and drawings on the walls and suspended by string from the ceiling would make the school "more like a kids' school." This led to an ongoing plan of action. A committee of six was formed to decorate the school. Time was provided each day for the group to hang their posters and drawings, all of which colorfully reflected what children prize and cherish. This was their public affirmation.

We believe that within each child is a dynamic force, a thrust, an urge to grow. Each one seeks personal identity. With troubled children this desire to become more is sometimes obscured by the many scars of failure and criticism, but even though this "will to be" is buried deep and often denied, it can be nourished in small intimate groups where children feel safety and trust.

STRATEGY NO. 5 —————————————————————————————

Charlie from outer space

As a group activity one day we told the story of a space craft from an unknown destination that had landed in our school yard. As the door of the space ship opened, there stood one lonely figure thought to be a child of about eleven. We asked the children to combine their imaginations and contribute their ideas of how the child might appear. They gave suggestions for a collective drawing that one of the teachers drew on a large portable blackboard. After finishing the drawing we asked the children to name this person from outer space. They called him Charlie.

We then asked them to role-play a situation with Charlie. One person sat behind the board and became Charlie's voice. One by one he called on the children to answer two questions:

What two things do you enjoy most about this world you live in?

What one or two harmful things he (Charlie) should try to avoid in the world.

Our children assured Charlie that he would enjoy watching TV, eating candy and cake, smelling flowers, kissing girls, and having a dog as a pet. They cautioned him against pills (narcotics), cigarettes, and beer which might "rust him on the inside."

As a followup activity the children in your class could be encouraged to write a letter of appreciation for all the enjoyable things they listed. It might also be appropriate to write letters of concern to those people responsible for the harmful things.

STRATEGY NO. 6 ———————————————————————
a penny for your thoughts

A simple strategy with a Lincoln copper penny[9] is a stimulating way to begin a discussion on values.

Each child is given a penny and asked to examine it closely to determine what cultural values are projected by the coin itself. They then share ideas of what we believe as a nation, such as:

1. "We revere and even enshrine men like Lincoln." Questions easily flow from such an observation. What were the qualities that made Lincoln a great leader? Do you know anyone like him living today? What would you like to be remembered for doing? Is there anyone in our world we should write to or call to express our appreciation for their human qualities?
2. "We trust in God." What are your beliefs about God? What is your God like? Do some people have different Gods? What do these others believe?
3. "We believe in liberty." What liberties do you prize in your life? What liberties would you like to possess? Are any people that you know personally denied liberty? What liberty or freedom have you lost over the past year? What ones have you gained?

Another, even more basic use of the Lincoln penny is to give the children each a coin and have them imagine it as an ancient coin representing a past, lost generation of people. From the coin ask the children to deduct what that ancient civilization might have been like, have known, or might have believed, such as:

Men wore beards then.

They had a calendar, a God, buildings.

They knew how to mine minerals and mint coins.

They had a language with words; they could print.

They "trusted" and must have valued "liberty."

They had developed a numbers system.

After the discussion each child is allowed to keep the penny as a reminder of some of the values that nations of people believe important enough to imprint upon their coins. Foreign coins can also be used to learn the values other people in other countries cherish.

[9]This idea was given to us by Bob Zach, Resource Teacher, Language Arts for the Poudre R-1 schools, Fort Collins, Colorado.

As a followup exercise, we sometimes ask the children to design a coin that conveys what our small school culture believes. What things, people, and words would we include in the coins we would mint? This exercise adapts itself easily to expression in either drawing the coin or molding it in clay.

In these small ways children are introduced to the beliefs of their world, their nation, and their immediate school community. They are not admonished to believe or obey these traditions but only to realize there are values that people have been willing to live for and even die for in order to insure their preservation.

STRATEGY NO. 7

future worlds

In 1997—only twenty years from now—our children will have grown through adolescence into young adulthood. Most of them will be in their late twenties. In this strategy we asked two boys, Jim and Mark, ages 11 and 12, to imagine what their world would be like in twenty years.

> Where will they live?
>
> What will they eat?
>
> What will they do for recreation and work?
>
> What will they talk about?
>
> Will the world be a good place to live? Why or why not?
>
> What do they imagine they personally will be doing as a vocation in that future world of 1997.

These questions were posed a day before our regular group meeting in order to give the boys time to develop their ideas before presenting them to the group.

The next day they told the group how they envisioned the world of the future:

"We will all live under huge glass domes to protect us from foul weather and disease. The domes will direct solar energy into our homes and factories. We will eat all kinds of pills that will give us the proper nutrition. We will travel by unirail commuter trains or personal jet packs that fit on our backs and enable us to fly anywhere within the dome. For recreation we will enjoy flying by jet pack, walking through museums of how the world once was, and taking walks outside the dome. Computers will be helping us solve the problems of living with each other and establishing better relations with other planets. Life will be easy and good because people will be healthier and live longer." Jim thought he would like to work with the giant computer because he's good at math and Mark would enjoy being one of the museum guides because he likes people.

The boys then carried on a dialogue between themselves about their life in 1997 and later the children reacted to their presentation with questions and comments. In this way we entered the fantasy world of children and became acquainted with both their hopes and their fears—veiled fears of regimentation, of a sterile and passive life-style. Yet in this fantasy world there was hope for happiness, healthful living, and meaningful work. In this way we hoped to point out the idea that as people change the environment, they too must change.

SIX

feelings--emotions

In achieving health and well-being, each day our bodies automatically complete many physical cycles. We wake up in the morning, stretch, yawn, and fill our lungs with air. We hold our breath for a moment to expand our chest. Then we release in a full cycle of breathing. This action invigorates our heart, which also fills, holds momentarily, then releases its life-giving flow. The digestive process begins with a desire for eating, then assimilation, and later elimination. In these living processes of life, respiration, circulation, digestion, and even reproduction, there is a rhythm of *fill—hold—release*.[1] Quietly, smoothly, automatically, our body sees each process through to completion in its need for closure. Interruption of this three-fold cycle at any point causes complications, malfunctioning, and ill health. Choking, heart failure, constipation, and premature birth are some of the results. Thus, completion is a very important phenomenon in life.

This fill–hold–release process is also apparent on an emotional level. Which one of us has not experienced our nervous system being filled and flooded with anger, then the discomfort of being forced to hold that anger, and restraining against the pressure that strains to be released! How many times have we wanted to cry but instead choked back the tears? How many times have we sought to reach out tenderly and lovingly to touch someone but felt blocked for some reason? At these times we have experienced emotional constipation and have discovered that "holding on" is the best way to get "hung up" and "stuck" with an emotion. In addition, repression is the best way to magnify a given emotion so that even small, unexpressed angers can become rage. Collected moments of sadness can deteriorate into depression. Even stock-piled bits of tenderness can accumulate to become compulsive overprotection. We must recognize that completion of emotion through expression is not only necessary but healthy.

There is a pervasive denial of feeling in our society. Nowhere is emotional discharge encouraged. Even in dark movie houses people who cry during heartbreaking scenes receive many looks of disgust. Strange, indeed, when the intent of the writer, producer, and actors was to produce and heighten the emotion of sadness. Do we realize we thus encourage nonempathy? Children learn quite early that they better not pout, better not cry. Why? Even Santa Claus does not condone emotional release and humanness. In fact, the old "gentleman," not-so-gently, punishes those who release their uncomfortable feelings. It is no wonder

---

[1]This idea was given to us by Hugh Riordan, *Psyche Incorporated*, Wichita, Kansas.

we have produced many emotionally constipated children! So many children are hurting badly but are afraid to tell, are frustrated but cannot scream, are lonely yet cannot reach out in love. They are stuck with feelings of deep disappointment, inadequacy, and hurt, so they retreat into themselves seeking out hiding places. They feel cut off and alone, a heavy price to pay for uncertain safety. At other times when the unexpressed feelings of rage hurt too much, they strike out in explosive aggressiveness. Moderation is unknown to repressed children until they are taught that it is better to have several, small, mini-explosions than one, big, devastating, inappropriate maxi-explosion; better to release in spurts than in blasts.

In the next seven strategies we deal with emotions in a setting where we can help children become more aware that to be fully human is to feel all kinds of emotions.

1. Story Retell (a technique for lending support and empathy)
2. Emotion—Feelings—Awareness (to expand awareness to an array of human emotions)
3. Expressing Anger (exploring personal ways to dissipate anger)
4. What About Sunshine and Dreams? (feeling warm and happy)
5. Improvisations and Role-Playing (helping children go beyond catharsis to resolution and solution)
6. Fantastic Voyage (releasing emotional tension)
7. Vultures (coping with peer put-downs)

STRATEGY NO. 1
story retell (Jimmy and the Butterfly)

In one of our later strategies, "Words are important," one of our boys, nine years old, was confused by the word "pervert," a word that some cruel high-school students called all of the children who waited for the special education bus. Our boy thought to be perverted meant to be pregnant. Clearly this needed to be clarified, so we talked through the meaning of these words and then discussed alternative ways of coping with the name-calling high-school students:

1. Report the incident to the principal.
2. Call them "pervert" in turn.
3. Tell the bus driver.
4. Ignore them.
5. Request that the bus driver pick up students at a different location away from the high school.

6. Risk asking *one* high-school student not to call them names.

Our students entertain no fantasy that life is easy and that frustration is not a part of life. They have learned that there are risks in expressing one's feelings, but that there are appropriate times to do this. Our boy assumed responsibility by asking one high-school student in the gang not to hurt him or his friends anymore with their names. It worked! The high-school boy listened and then "cooled" his gang.

When our students tell us stories from their lives, we sometimes reply by telling them another story. This is how "Jimmy and the Butterfly" came to be. One of the authors composed it and then taped it for the next group meeting. Retelling a story has been a useful strategy with our children, a form of bibliotherapy, but more direct and personal.

Jimmy and the Butterfly

Thinking back I guess everyone was right when they said, "Jimmy is different." That is what was said when Jimmy first went to school. Teachers would shake their heads and say, "There's something different about Jimmy." And when you would ask them what is different they would answer, "He's so quiet and shy." "He seems afraid, and he daydreams a lot."

It wasn't long before the children began to notice Jimmy too. At recess he would wander over to the edge of the playground where weeds grew. He discovered trails where red ants brought seeds and other things into their den deep in the ground. Once he found a cricket and learned how it chirped by ruffling it's wings together. And there were always big orange monarch butterflies sailing by.

The day he brought a black, fuzzy caterpillar to class and allowed it to crawl up his arm and over his shoulder one of the children said, "He's crazy about bugs!"

"Jimmy, take that thing outdoors where you got it," scolded the teacher. Jimmy searched the weed patch until he found a broad leaf and then he gently placed the caterpillar there. "Crazy about bugs, crazy about bugs"—that phrase and the way it was said kept going over and over in Jimmy's mind.

Then it happened! Jimmy would never forget the day. "He's crazy all right," a child remarked. "Yeah, crazy and buggy." Up to this time the children had left Jimmy pretty much alone. Now they began calling him "Crazy Jimmy" and "Bug Boy"—"Here, bug boy."

Others added two words they had overheard their big brothers in high school use: "Retard!" "Pervert!"

Only when they said the words, they made them sound real cruel by almost singing the syllables: "Ree–tard!" "Per–vert!"

Jimmy felt lonelier and sadder than he had ever felt before. But he always held on to one hope. That just because the words were bad, he was not bad—even if other people thought he was!

Now the teachers on the playground began to notice Jimmy. "He's isolating himself," they would say. "Withdrawing." These were big words Jimmy didn't understand, but he would admit he was "keeping to himself," even hiding, trying to protect himself from those words that children threw at him like rocks. The words hurt even more than rocks, somehow.

That reminds me, there was something else about Jimmy that was different. There was one pocket in his jeans, the right pocket, I believe, that was always filled with something. "It's rocks," the children said, "He's got rocks in his head and in his pockets. Ha! Ha! Ha! I bet he'd like to throw them at us!" But no one really knew for sure and no one, at that time, ever got close enough to ask, "Whatcha got in your pocket, Jimmy?" No, no one ever got that close to Jimmy.

Then one day everything began to happen very quickly. Jimmy was on a bus going to another school. "Where you can get help," his parents said. "You'll like it there."

The new school was different (there's that word again, different), not like other schools. It was a small school and it just looked friendly and warm. Jimmy had remembered feeling "different," but now he began to realize that maybe being different wasn't so bad after all. In fact it felt real good.

Jimmy collected as many caterpillars as he wanted to at the new, small school, only here they seemed to prize them. The teachers put them in a room called the "Pet Center" to live along with lizards, hamsters, a yellow cat, and a huge number of fish. Every day the children fed and cared for the animals while Jimmy brought fresh leaves for his caterpillars. Then one morning it happened. The jars were filled with cocoons and inside each of them the caterpillars were sleeping.

Oh, I'm reminded of something else that happened on Jimmy's first day at the new school. One of the teachers asked, "Jimmy, what's in your right pocket?" Jimmy reached in and proudly laid out on the ground eight arrowheads. They were part of his collection that he had found by the river where he lived. Oh, it felt good to be able to share a part of his life with others.

In the spring the children watched a small hole appear in each of the cocoons. The butterflies were preparing to come out. Miracles happened as one by one the cases opened and beautiful wings began to unfold. "Let's take them outside in the sunshine," the teacher said. "Yes, let's let them be free," Jimmy added.

The children opened the jars and suddenly there was a blur of orange and black as the butterflies lifted themselves into the warm spring air. "They're free," the children cried, "free. Aren't they beautiful?"

Jimmy was smiling.

"Yes, they're free," thought Jimmy.

"Free like me,

free to be different,

and beautiful!"

STRATEGY NO. 2 ————————————————
emotion—feelings—awareness

Gestalt therapy maintains that we are so busy thinking that most of our vital energy is directed toward and used up in our heads; we consequently forget how to feel with our bodies. This is unfortunate, since we do not learn with the brain alone. Intelligence encompasses the total organism, thoughts as well as feelings. We are interested in feelings because most of the particular children we work with seem especially cut off from this basic function. They sometimes laugh and smile inappropriately when they are hurt, and they are not always aware of the full gamut of human emotion. They know fear, anger, anxiety, confusion, disappointment, guilt, loneliness, and rejection, but seldom do they recognize or feel joy, love, respect, confidence, trust, freedom, or acceptance.

We hope in this strategy to unwrap children's feelings and increase their awareness so they can better understand their world and experience more of what is reality.

We first asked the children to sit quietly with their eyes closed and take a journey into their bodies to explore and discover how they felt. They were advised that feelings can be located in the body and that when we feel we can usually point to a place where we feel sad, angry, hurt, or happy. After this excursion into inner space, our children reported feeling "happy, sleepy, sad, bad, mad, and dumb."

To discover even more feelings and emotions, we asked each child to cut out a picture from a magazine given to them (one magazine per child to eliminate confusion) that reflected a feeling or mood. Each then pasted this picture on a tagboard and returned to the group circle to ask the other children what feeling they saw in the picture. The children recognized happiness, excitement, joy, sadness, anger, thoughtfulness, fear, guilt, cruelty, disappointment, and hope.

Several children then were asked to remember a time in their life when they had experienced one of these emotions. How did they feel? How did their feeling affect others around them? How can children break up bad feelings and feel better? (If we can recognize a feeling, we can choose the alternatives that can make us feel better.)

We then circulated around the group pausing at different people to ask, "How do you think this person is feeling now? How can you know how they feel? What are good ways to treat a person who feels this way?" (Alternatives and action.) As an example, one of the teachers was "exhausted" from late hours. The students recognized this and were asked how they could relate to a teacher who is tired and exhausted. "Don't bug him," "Stay out of his way," "Do our work when he asks us," were their remarks.

We used three followup activities for this session:

1. We played records that conveyed a variety of moods and asked the children how the music made them feel. We asked them to move their bodies according to the theme or mood of the music.

2. A "collage of feelings" was constructed using magazine pictures with the pictures projecting various feelings. The children then identified with the pictures that best reflected their feelings at the time.

    Another use of the "collage of feelings" is in anticipation of doing something special, for example, going on a weekend or perhaps going home for Thanksgiving or getting ready for Christmas (holidays provide good opportunities for anticipation). The children begin by deciding what picture they want most to experience during the holiday, weekend, or vacation, and then, as a group, they brainstorm a whole list of activities that will help them accomplish the particular feeling they desire—that happy face—that excitement—whatever it was. The children brainstorming ideas for their own family will give alternatives to the other children.

    When the children come back from an experience, they go to the "collage of feelings" and establish what was the feeling of the actual experience. Then we brainstorm after the fact about some of the things they might have done to change that feeling if they had experienced disappointment. In this way the children begin to learn the notion "we can shape our lives. We are in charge of our lives and the next time we go to do something like that, we can have it come out better than it may have this time."

3. In still another strategy a feeling line was drawn on newsprint and taped to the wall where children could locate their feelings when they came to school in the morning. They placed their name card on the appropriate emotion.

angry	shy	afraid	hurt	lonely	affectionate	bored	sad	happy
				Susie			Joe	

   In this simple way we are saying to our children "It's okay to be visible. Let us know how you feel. Perhaps we can help if you feel 'lonely,' Susie; perhaps, Joe, we can enter into your 'happy' mood and celebrate the joy with you today." Sidney Jourard wrote about self-disclosure and proposed it might be "that people become clients because they have not disclosed themselves in some optimum degree to the people in their life."[2]

4. At follow-up sessions we ask:

How do you feel most of the time?

How do most kids feel?

[2]Jourard, Sidney, *The Transparent Self*, Van Nostrand Reinhold, New York, 1964, p. 21.

How would you like to feel?

How can we lose unhappy feelings?

How can we sustain joyfulness?

These sessions afford many opportunities for role playing, fantasy trips, clay molding, and mime work.

Our children have been especially receptive to mime work. Musical accompaniment helps them overcome their inhibitions as they act out stories and move their bodies like clouds dashing over the blue Caribbean Ocean or floating lazily over summer meadows, or like trees in a windstorm, or like a hawk circling the sky. They tug-of-war without a rope, pulling, miming the many positions. Sometimes one team lets go of the rope and the other team tumbles backwards. There is lots of laughter in this activity which helps children express feelings of both anger and joy through their bodies.

STRATEGY NO. 3

expressing anger (verbally plus total body)

In the previous strategy we alluded to the themes of aggression that frequently occur in the projections of the children. "I would be a tiger because they could eat all the other animals." "I would be a wild horse and kick people." "I'd be an elephant and trample anything that got in my way." These unpleasant feelings clog the free flow of life in many of our children. At times, their resentments and anger seem to dominate their energy, thought, and action. The expression of resentment and anger both verbally and through body experience has made life much better for some of the children.

One verbal method we have used is to team two children together as partners. One child then maintains eye contact and listens to his or her partner repeat a series of *"no's"* in as many different ways as the verbalizing partner can. The silent, listening partner does not react except to just be there and give support with warm, attentive eyes.

Each child is usually given two minutes to express the *"no's"* and then the other partner is given a turn while the first child reciprocates by listening. After both partners have participated, they sit together and talk for a few more minutes about the times they said, "no" and the times when they needed to say, "no."

They then repeat the cycle again. This time, after each "no" the child takes time to briefly explain the situation in his or her life where a "no" is needed. The child says another "no" and explains what that is about. We usually stop with each child saying "no" three times with a short explanation.

During the first round the children are into the spirit of what it means to say "no." This has the effect of charging them up emotionally for the second round. In the second round their "*no's*" are more definite and clear, reflecting what they need to do in their real lives.

We usually demonstrate this technique to the children to give them some idea as to how the different "*no's*" might sound. Imagine doing it yourself: You say, "no" and then you say "Nooooo," and then you say "NO, NO, NO" as you hit your hand on the table. Your responses to "no" build quite gradually in two minutes. We found the children did not imitate because they have their own personal material about "no" that comes out very quickly.

We have also used total body experience by pounding on a large punching bag or pillow placed on the floor. Pounding is an effective way for some children to express their anger. In this activity the child is allowed to scream, yell, use words, or make any other sound the pounding evokes. The child hits until the anger has been worked through.

There are some cautions in using this technique of converting angry feelings into total body experience because some children become overly stimulated with pounding and never seem to obtain closure. For these children the technique is not recommended.

We have asked our children to suggest personal ways they have found effective in draining off anger. They use various forms: tearing paper, throwing rocks at trees or walls, yelling, swinging, kicking cans, talking, smashing clay, pounding nails in a log, throwing bean bags. We encourage all of these and suggest talking as one of the better methods. There are three lines from John Steinbeck's book, *The Grapes Of Wrath*, which fit our own experience. Casey, one of the characters, says, "Yes, you should talk, he said. Sometimes a sad man can talk the sadness right out through his mouth. Sometimes a killin' man can talk the murder right out of his mouth an' not do no murder."[3] Some of our children have experienced this as truth.

STRATEGY NO. 4 ——————————————

what about sunshine and dreams?

Psychological studies have shown that when people remember and think about words like, *love, peace, joy, laughter, music,* and *sunshine,* feelings of

---

[3]Steinbeck, John, *The Grapes of Wrath,* Viking Press, New York, 1939, p. 45.

happiness are stimulated. From time to time it may be helpful to inventory what or who makes us happy and where we experience our own personal happiness. An awareness of these things can lead to a commitment on our part to include more of these happy experiences in our lives.

John Denver is a young musician who wrote a song about sunshine and how it made him feel. He wrote it one gray, cold wintery day in Minnesota when snow covered the fields. He remembered back to the yellow, summer days and the way sunshine warmed his shoulders making him happy.

To begin this group activity we play the song, "Sunshine On My Shoulders," by John Denver, from the album, "Poems, Prayers, and Promises" (RCA Stereo Records), or we read the lyrics of his song as a poem. The words reflect warm human emotions of happiness, joy, and ecstacy.

We then ask the students to close their eyes and think of one word that makes them feel happy. As they get in touch with these happy thoughts we ask them to write their word on a piece of paper (the teacher can do this for younger children who cannot yet write or spell) and then make a drawing suggested by their word.

After the children finish their drawings, they share the word and the picture they drew with the group. All drawings are then posted on the walls as a continued stimulus to memories, thoughts, and feelings of happiness and well-being.

One child chose the word "flowers" because, "Flowers have pretty colors and smell good." She then drew a picture of one large, colorful flower. A boy said, trucks made him happy. "I like the noise they make as they go down the highway." He drew a semi-truck. A drawing of trees with apples reminded another child of "autumn" because "It's the time of year with lots of color and ripe apples." "I drew cats playing because cats always seem so happy." "I thought of the word 'love' so I drew a boy and a girl with large red valentine hearts because when you're in love you can go steady." "Home is my word so I drew this house with a large backyard. Sometime I'd like to have a backyard like this with a well, a fence, and a yard light."

(An Open Letter)

Dear John (Denver)

Thanks for writing so many happy songs, simple enough for children to understand. The "sunshine" you write about along with the "dreams" of children make us high.

Warmly,
Sid and Bob

STRATEGY NO. 5 ——————————————————
improvisation and role-playing

As we have written in previous pages, we want our children to become aware of their feelings, know the impact of the various emotions of their body and behavior, and be able to express their emotions appropriately to experience release. One way to complete the cycle from awareness to expression and resolution is to invent situations that cause emotional reactions in children. These situations are easily identified on the playground and in the classroom along with other life happenings.

We begin by asking the children to "freeze" the facial expressions on their faces while we pass a mirror around so they can see the outward projections of inner emotions as the emotions crinkle their eyes, line their foreheads, and turn their mouths. We then ask volunteers to react to other invented events. This time we ask them to mobilize their whole body for these reactions to see where the tension develops.

> You have just been told to shut up!
> You have just learned that school will be out for three days and you can go on a trip anyplace you like.
> You really think you've fallen in love.
> You've been putting it off for a long time but now you have to face up to some difficult problem.
> All you ever seem to do is fail and make mistakes.
> Someone just hit you and called you "stupid."
> Tonight is your birthday party and many friends are coming over to help you celebrate.
> You have just been told by your father you are grounded for three weeks for misplacing one of his tools.

After the children have frozen into complete bodily reactions to these situations, we ask them to improvise a dialogue with one other person and act out these situations. As each pair role-plays, the other students watch and listen and after the dialogue suggest other alternatives.

We have only suggested a few situations of role-playing; we suggest your own students can best create their own particular emotionally packed scenes from their individual experiences.

STRATEGY NO. 6 ———————————————————
fantastic voyage

In our last strategy we stressed the importance of helping children go beyond catharsis. Many children need further help with emotions because for so long they have repressed or held these emotions tightly in their muscles and bones. William Schutz wrote, "Implicit general recognition of the close connection between the emotional and the physical is evident in the verbal idioms that have developed in social interaction."[4] We have adapted a partial list of terms from his book that "describe behavior and feelings in bodily terms."[5]

"Sorehead"—many of our children have headaches.

"Shoulder a burden"—their shoulders are rounded; their chests concave.

"Grit your teeth"—jaw muscles knot in tension as they grit and grind.

"Butterflies in the stomach"—some are good candidates for ulcers.

"Broken hearted"—these become apathetic and depressed.

"Big mouth"—their bluster covers insecurity.

"My aching back"—shoulder and back muscles are tense and hard.

"Thin-skinned"—ultra sensitive to anything they perceive as criticism—They can take no more.

"Pissed-Off"—they go to the bathroom often or are incontinent and enuretic.

Schutz and others believe that the bones and muscles of the body, become set and fixed after years and years of repression and tension, that "some muscles shorten and thicken, others become immobilized by consolidation of the tissue involved."[6] These kinds of children are not free to move with grace and freedom.

In the next section of our book we will discuss several tension-reducing strategies. Now we would like to deal with specific areas where children tend to hold tension.

We begin our "Fantastic Voyage" by asking the children to lie on their backs and close their eyes so that they can concentrate better. We then ask them to imagine they are in a small capsule traveling around their own bodies looking for tense, sore, tired, hurt places. We suggest areas to explore very slowly and methodically: the *head* first, the eyes, the

---

[4]Schutz, William C., *Joy, Expanding Human Awareness*, Grove Press, New York, 1967, p. 25.
[5]Ibid, pp. 25–26.
[6]Ibid, p. 27.

mouth, the jaws, forehead, ears, cheeks, chin; then the *neck* and throat into the *shoulders* across the big muscles down into the *arms*, the elbows, wrists, hands, fingers; back up to the *chest*, the lungs, the breathing, ribs, back; now the *stomach*, stop all along the way to examine for tightness, soreness, hurt; down each *leg*, first the right leg, the thigh, knee, calf, ankle, foot, toes; back up again and down the left leg, upper part, lower, the feet and toes.

We then ask the children to tell us where each of them was aware of tension. They tell us their most common stress points are eyes, shoulders, chest, and legs. This becomes the order of our relaxation time.

We begin by turning off the lights and relieving the eyes. We provide a damp washcloth for each child to place over his or her eyes. The coolness of the cloth is maintained by turning it over from time to time. After a few minutes we remove the cloths and move on to the shoulders. The children can continue to close their eyes or open them if this is more comfortable.

We now ask the children to hunch their shoulders as high as they can. This is done slowly and maintained at the extreme position for a few seconds. Then we tell them to slowly lower their shoulders so they sink into the floor. They rest for a while and then repeat the process three or four times. This greatly reduces tension and improves posture as well.

The chest is relaxed through breathing. We first ask each child to concentrate on his breathing rhythm without trying to change it in any way. When each child has been made aware of an easy rhythm, we ask them to slowly breath in, filling their lungs to capacity, holding the breath for a moment, and then slowly allowing the release of breath through the nostrils. We usually fill to a count of eight, hold for four, then release for a count of eight. After this is done four times, we ask the children to again slip into an easy, rhythmic breathing. We ask them to notice any tension that has invaded either the eyes or the shoulders. We help them again to release the tension from these areas by simply suggesting to them quietly, "Relax the eyes, ease out the tension, be quiet, soften the shoulders, letting them grow loose and relaxed, and keep both eyes and shoulders easy, relaxed, soft."

Continuing to work through the entire body, we move to the legs, asking the children to stretch their right legs by pretending they are pointing to something with their toes. We tense each leg three times and allow it, after the tension, to limply relax onto the floor.

We then play quiet music for another five or six minutes, while again suggesting the children relax their eyes, their shoulders, their breathing, and their legs by repeating to themselves inaudibly, "Rest —relax—be calm." After a period of music we ask them to sit up slowly, come awake, and then stand loose for a moment or two. Invariably after these relaxation periods the general mood of the children is quiet and subdued. They talk more quietly and move more softly and with consideration for others around them. In this way, we propose to reduce tensions daily that have built up over the years. For extremely tense children we suggest practicing this procedure at home as well as those procedures that follow in our next section.

STRATEGY NO. 7 ————————————————
vultures

Every child in our school, without exception, came to us with a brain, a body, and a vulture. The brain and body are apparent but the vulture is unseen by the casual observer; nevertheless these big birds are hidden deep in the psyche (soul) of each child. Trained vulture spotters can detect the presence of these birds of prey quite easily because vultures feed on the self-esteem of all of us—adults as well as children. They pick and chew at the personal core of every human being. The symptoms of vultures are feelings of fatigue, fright, and defeat. It has been concluded after careful observation and study that vultures are nourished by put-downs and killer statements. Every time a child is called "stupid," or "retard," or "weird," the vulture increases in size—the bigger the vulture, the smaller the self-concept becomes. We warn our children against vultures and against feeding them by taunting others with killer and put-down statements.

Marianne Simon recently wrote several successful strategies for killing vultures and the hurtful emotions they create by depriving the ugly birds of their natural food: put-downs and killer statements. She suggests students keep "Put-Down Journals"[7] in which they record all the put-downs and killer statements they hear in one day. Teachers are encouraged to keep journals too. Children then read these statements to the group to increase their awareness of these damaging statements.

As a followup, the children are asked to keep a page on how they feel when someone zaps them with a killer statement. They are asked to consider what kind of feelings are created in them: sadness, anger, hurt, despair, numbness? If possible, they are asked to consider what specific part of the body reacted most to the hurt: their head, stomach, or heart? (We have written about the connection between tissue and emotions, between a headache, a stomach pain, and the feelings that produced it.)

[7]Simon, Marianne, "Chasing Killer Statements from the Classroom," *Learning*, Aug./Sept. 1975, p. 80.

At this point it is useful to consider the mixed responses one might have to a killer statement. "Did you want to cry, run, fight back, scream, hide?"

Finally, Marianne asks that a "moratorium" on killer statements be declared, if even for just an hour or a day, after which children are asked to discuss their reaction to the moratorium. Students always report with sighs and smiles of relief.

"It was really neat."

"It felt good."

(We always ask students to substitute "I" for "it" to bring about more personal meaning so that the former "it" statements become:

"(It) *I* was really neat"

"(It) *I* felt good"

In this way students learn to shrink their vultures and in time even eliminate them because vultures cannot tolerate statements of validation!

SEVEN

touching and validating

"Every person has the need to be touched and to be recognized by other people . . ."[1] Yet we live in a society that is quite closed and reserved in both touch and recognition. Sidney Jourard wrote, "I believe we are a nation of people who are starved for physical contact."[2] He wondered about ". . . men or women who have never been touched, or hugged, or have never been in intimate body contact with others. Could we say that their bodies have not come to life, that their bodies do not exist in a phenomenological sense?"[3] He wrote from conviction, "The therapist of the future ultimately will learn from that unheeded prophet, Reich, and become less afraid to get into meaningful physical contact with his patient . . ."[4]

We applaud a famous Japanese sculptor who "once confounded the curators of an American art gallery where his works were being shown. At the base of each statue the sculptor has placed a polite little sign that reads: 'Please Touch'."[5]

We touch our children!

Touch, we believe, is therapeutic.

Touch is calming . . .

Touch is loving . . .

We "get in touch." . . .

Our validation of children is akin to what Jourard speaks of as "faith." He writes that instead of "dispairing with a patient . . . and pursue all the roots of 'pathology' in him, I immediately begin to wonder how it would be possible to mobilize his spirit or his capacity to transcend the present circumstances that he has let grind him down. Maybe over the years I've just become more effective at communicating my faith in their potentials . . . or maybe I've become more effective at infecting patients with the seeds of faith in themselves. A patient will say, 'You seem to have faith in me, so I looked, and I found faith in myself.' Maybe

[1]James, Muriel, and Dorothy Jongeward, *Born To Win: Transactional Analysis with Gestalt Experiments*, Addison-Wesley, Boston, 1971, p. 44.
[2]Jourard, Sidney M., *Disclosing Man to Himself*, Van Nostrand Reinhold, New York, 1968, p. 65.
[3]Ibid, p. 66.
[4]Ibid, p. 67.
[5]McMahon, Edwin M., and Peter A. Campbell, *Please Touch*, Sheed and Ward, Mission, Kansas, 1969, p. 1.

this is the factor in iatrogenic wellness— the strength of the healer's faith in the potentials of the sufferer to transcend the limiting conditions of his existence."[6]

We have included in our strategies for touch and validation:

1. Touch—Caring
2. From Head to Toes (to reduce skin hunger by receiving and giving gentle touch)
3. Invitations (strengthening validation for growth)
4. Animals I Like (discovering new possibilities for being in the world)
5. Good News Letters (more specific recognition based on achievement)
6. It's OK to Be You (Hey, we're all OK)
7. Lunch Box Notes (a simple way for parents to build self-esteem in their children)

Love as experienced through touch and validation breaks down feelings of loneliness and isolation in children. The above strategies provide warm, friendly ways for children to interact with each other. They further provide suggestions for teachers and parents to fulfill the love and esteem needs of children.

STRATEGY NO 1 ——————————————————————————

touch—caring

> *If you touch me soft and gentle*
> *If you look at me and smile at me*
> *If you listen to me talk sometimes before you talk*
> *I will grow, really grow.*
> > *Bradley (Age 9)[7]*

Every human being suffers some degree of "skin hunger." Each needs to be touched in soothing, relaxing, healing ways. Touch is perhaps still the best way to validate another person because touch shows care. It is an art to care for another person responsibly in this way. Children especially need to be able to receive as well as give soft, gentle, caressing touches, and in this way know they are loved and capable of loving others.

We have developed and outlined a procedure to use with children in helping them to nonverbally express caring:

[6]Jourard, *op. cit.*, p. 59.
[7]From James and Jongeward, *Born To Win*, p. 44.

1. The children stand in a circle with their hands comfortably on another child's shoulder. They each then give their partner a soothing neck-shoulder massage.

2. (A nonverbal exercise) While the children are still standing, ask them each to choose a partner. When this is done the taller partner will be designated *blue* because this person is nearer the sky; the shorter partner will be designated *green* since he or she is closer to the grass. The greens close their eyes while the blues get a chair and place it directly behind the greens. The blues touch their green partner on the shoulder as a signal to sit. The greens then sit down without opening their eyes, showing they trust their partner to place the chairs properly. The blues now begin to gently massage the temples, foreheads, and necks of the greens. At a nonverbal signal from the teacher (a snap of the finger) the blues kneel in front of their partner. The greens slowly open their eyes and look at the person who massaged them. The blues then pick a new green partner, massage, kneel in front, etc. The blues continue to massage greens until they have done so to every green. At this time the blues are switched and the greens begin the massaging in the same way by placing the chair, then massaging each blue in the circle.

3. Greens now lay on their stomachs while the blues give them backrubs and back scratches. Blues move from green to green as the teacher snaps his or her finger. The blues then trade with greens to receive their backrubs and back scratches. An interesting variation that all children seem to love is the bear walk. In this massage the heels of the hands are used in a firm pressing motion across the shoulders and back, as if a big bear were walking. The slow pressure and then release sooths and relaxes the deep muscles of the back.

4. Have all the children lie down in a comfortable position. While they are relaxing ask them to respond to these questions by thinking the answers to themselves:

   Who touches you?

   How do they touch you?

   How would you like to be touched?

   Can you ask them to touch you in ways you enjoy?

   Whom do you touch?

   How do you usually touch others?

   Could you begin touching others more gently?

5. Encourage the children to ask for and give touch throughout the day as another way of validating a person.

We have discovered that forms of tapping or other light massage tend to make our children more tense and hyper. A firm touch seems to be the most beneficial. Caution children never to tickle their partner as this destroys trust and the relaxing we are trying to achieve.

Several of our children need training in the healing touch. At this time in their lives they are incapable of extending themselves in gentle, loving touch.

Some children react defensively to touch and fear it. Perhaps they have been touched only in anger and so they shrink from human touch. Gradually all of our children are responding willingly to the sharing of touch. We try to include touch–caring on a daily basis.

Harvey Jakins, the originator of reevaluation counseling suggests that each person requires a minimum of four hugs each day to survive. It is a good idea to schedule "hug days" so that all fill their quota and satisfy their own "skin hunger."

STRATEGY NO. 2 ────────────────────────────────
from head to toes

Another way to touch "soft and gentle" is to group the children in a room where they can lie on their backs on the floor. We ask which children are feeling really worn out and tired. These children are permitted to be first in receiving "head caring." They lie down, close their eyes, and begin to relax while the other children each choose one of the tired persons to massage. The massage begins with the teacher suggesting the following method in a quiet, comforting voice:

> Softly rub the forehead of this tired person. Smooth out all the tension. With your fingers ease out all the tiredness. Do this very quietly and gently several times.

> Now, with both hands massage the back of the neck and the shoulders, and the base of the head. Softly, smoothly massage out all the tight feeling in those areas. This time massage the sides of the neck. Your touch will help the person relax and feel good. Work under the chin now, softly, gently. Now massage across their cheeks and again back to their foreheads, easing them, quieting them, relaxing them.

> Now gently let your fingertips touch their eyelids. Your fingers will feel cool and calming, helping them to release all the tension. Do this several times.

> Quietly bend over now and whisper your name in their ear so they will know who cared for them. Move on and choose another person. (At no time during this period do the children lying down open their eyes.)

After changing three or four times, the people lying down are asked to slowly wake up, open their eyes, and quietly sit up and relax for a few minutes more.

Those who have been administering the head caring now lie down to receive it and the process is repeated.

On another day we introduce the foot massage. It begins with the children scrubbing their own feet with a washrag they have brought from home. This in itself is envigorating and insures clean feet for the next massage strategy.

Again one group of children lie on their backs with their eyes closed. They are told to begin to relax by letting the weight of their bodies be held by the floor.

The soothing voice of the teacher suggests the method as each child receives a partner for the massage:

> First of all with both your hands squeeze all parts of your partner's right foot. Squeeze firmly and then release. As you release, the tight muscles of the feet and ankles will begin to relax. Do this several times across the arches, more gently on the toes, the sides of the foot, the ankles, over and over again.
>
> Now with your fingers, firmly massage the foot. Don't tickle. Make your touch firm and steady. Pretend the foot is clay and you are molding it, firming it. This will feel very good to your partner. Continue now to experiment with your own way of bringing relaxation to this tired right foot.
>
> Now bend over and whisper your name in your partner's ear. Then choose another person to relax, this time work on that person's left foot.

After the children have had both feet massaged, they slowly rise, relax, and then help those who have been giving foot massages to them.

When both strategies have been introduced we sometimes combine the two, beginning first with the heads and then proceeding later to the feet. The general effect of these strategies is to reduce general tension and tightness and to help the children feel more cared for, vital, and alive!

STRATEGY NO. 3 —————————————————
invitations

> *LOVE*
> *has a way of wondering about*
> *deep potentials in each of*
> *us we never dreamed*
> *we possessed.*
>
> *LOVE*
> *invites us to forget for*
> *a time who and what we*
> *think we are and*
> *consider what we*
> *might become.*

> *LOVE*
> *encourages us to transcend*
> *old ways of being*
> *in the world.*
> *LOVE IS*
> *a wonder–er,*
> *an inviter*
> *and encourager.*
> *IN LOVE'S*
> *warming, each of*
> *us can grow.*

Many children have been taught they should not think too much about themselves, let alone value and love who and what they are. They are told that thinking highly of self is a oneway street to snobbery and arrogance. There is for us another quite different aspect of love that allows for self-respect. Leo Buscaglia says it very well: "First of all a loving person has to care about himself. This is number one. I don't mean an ego trip. I'm talking about someone who really cares about himself, who says, 'Everything is filtered through me, and so the greater I am, the more I have to give. The greater knowledge I have, the more I'm going to have to give. The greater understanding I have, the greater is my ability to teach others and to make myself the most fantastic, the most beautiful, the most wondrous, the most tender human being in the world.' "[8]

In this strategy we invite our children to consider qualities they like about themselves . . . qualities that helped them feel, "I'm an OK person."

We ask each child to sit alone for a few minutes and choose one good thing about himself or herself. Each child was given a tagboard with the heading:

What's good about   (name)

When the children each discover one good thing about themselves, they affirm this attribute by writing it as number one on their poster.

What's good about   Sally

1. I think I am kind to animals.

The children then return to the group to show their posters and tell the group what they wrote about themselves. After they finish, the group is asked to close their eyes and think of other good things about each person. One child from the group is asked to volunteer a second positive statement and it is written on the poster. (We limit the comments to one child to insure that the activity moves quickly, enabling each child in the circle an equal opportunity to receive strengthening affirmation.)

Each person has a turn showing his or her poster and having one additional comment added. After the group has finished, each child then tapes the poster on the wall. The teacher encourages all the children to make additional sincere comments on all the posters throughout the week. The teacher helps those children who have difficulty expressing their ideas in writing and also participates by adding his or her own comments. At the end of the week the posters are reviewed and each child is asked to read his or her entire list of "good things."

[8]Buscaglia, Leo F., *Love*, Chas. B. Slack, Thorofare, New Jersey, 1972, p. 8.

The teacher or another student then reinforces the list by saying, for example: "Sally, we are all happy that you are kind to animals. We invite and encourage you to become even more loving toward them." After the invitations for each child have been extended, the children are asked to respond by saying, "Thank you for encouraging me."

Below is an example of one boy's poster after several children and teachers expanded his list:

What's good about John?

1. I am good at drawing trucks and trees.
2. You are friendly.
3. You are cool.
4. You are talking more.
5. You are a good artist.

John was invited to "draw more things—birds, flowers, people, houses, the whole world." He was encouraged to be "even more friendly, spontaneous, outgoing, and cool" and to talk with us because "we all enjoy his rap very much." He was invited to someday "join Michelangelo, DaVinci, and Picasso in the list of the world's greatest artists."

John exclaimed, "Wow, thanks for encouraging me."

When children consider their strengths, their weaknesses are eclipsed. Encouragement, support, and celebration of their attributes help them grow. That is *validation*!

Many times troubled children feel uncomfortable with validation. At first the validation is so foreign to them, not at all consistent with how they have come to view themselves. When you first tell a boy who has feelings of despair and disappointment that he is really a capable person, he may duck the well-intended compliment in what we have identified as the "dandruff syndrome"—a flicking off of the compliment as if it were unsightly dandruff.

It really is eerie to watch people receive compliments in our particular culture. They just don't know how to take a compliment. You tell someone that you find their blue tie beautiful and they'll say as quickly as they can, "Oh, and I love that blouse you're wearing." Or if you tell a specific teacher that you hear she is doing really nice things with her class, she'll say something like, "Oh, they're such nice children." The point is that we don't seem to let validation come naturally. Children and adults have to be trained to accept validation. The training is full of laughter and full of preposterous responses. For example, in our classes when we do validation, we have people respond with sentences like this, "How perceptive of you to notice," or "You sure do know beauty when you see it," or "Would you mind repeating that again?" Perhaps this last is the ultimate way to receive validation. When someone says something nice to you, you ask them, "Would you mind saying that once more so I can really hear it?" To do the dandruff flick is the equivalent of eating food and taking two bits and spitting it out. We need to train people to let the validation in so it can do the most benefit to their soul.

STRATEGY NO. 4 ─────────────────────────────
animals I like

Psychologists and philosophers have always found the subject of dreams, metaphor, and fantasy intriguing subjects for inquiry; each holding a potential for changing human personality. Some believe that if we can choose new, exciting metaphors for our lives, new constructs of what we might become, we can move our life in that direction and become what we fantasize.

Long before modern psychology, the American Indians intuitively knew about metaphors. They named their children after animals, hoping that the children would, during the course of their lives, attain some of the animal's attributes.

> The grace and speed of an antelope.
> The strength and courage of a bear.
> The wisdom and patience of the owl.

Children naturally identify with animals and project some of their own needs and concerns when asked to choose an animal they would like to be. This tendency for children to project can aid them in considering new metaphors for their lives. Perhaps from this a new identity can emerge.

In the group one day we asked the children to imagine what it would be like to be an animal—any animal.

For the most part the children viewed animals as strong, kind, loving, happy, independent, free, and sometimes angry. (The themes of strength, power, aggression, and freedom predominate, reflecting these children's present needs and values.)

We then asked them to choose one animal they would rather be than any other and tell why they chose that particular animal. Their choices were unique and fitting. One boy chose to be "a bird flying high in the sky" (freedom—even escape); another small boy preferred "tigers —because they could eat all the other animals" (domination and aggression); a girl, nearing termination and return to the regular classroom, said simply, "I'd like to be a kitten 'cause they're soft and nice" (she had become affectionate—tender—warm).

In the final part of the session each child was the focus person as teachers recognized each choice and validated each child with some positive attribute of the animal chosen. The teacher said to the boy who wanted to be a bird, "We know you would like to be more independent and free. We'll try to help you if you want us to." To the "tiger" the teacher responded, "It's tough to be small. You sometimes get shoved around. Maybe now the rest of the group understands your feeling and won't pick on you as much." To the "kitten" the comment was, "You have become a cuddly, warm, friendly person and we all like you very much."

Many of our children have been deprived of healthy, mature, sensitive adults with whom they can identify and use as models. Even on a recent national scale the three most "respected" men in America are Henry Kissinger, Billy Graham, and Gerald Ford—men too far removed from the lives of children. "Respectful" animals are much closer; so we, like the ancient prophet, do not hesitate to suggest, "go to the ant (or the bird, tiger, or kitten for that matter), study their ways and become wise."

There are many fascinating follow-through activities after the first session:

1. Choose different types of music (light versus heavy) and have all the light animals move in time, then all the heavies.
2. What happens when a "tiger" meets a "bird" for example. Have the children "act out" the meeting.
3. Draw pictures of their favorite animals or make a collage of many animals.
4. Study the various animals named by the children with an eye to the worthy attributes of each animal.
5. Devote several story hours to reading short stories about animals.

STRATEGY NO. 5
good news letters

We recently heard a story about Dr. David Cronk, principal at Faye Wright Elementary School in Salem, Oregon. Dr. Cronk requested students be sent to the principal's office when they have accomplished something worthy of recognition during the week. The students sign a guest book and talk about their contribution while Dr. Cronk rewards them with a piece of cake. If their accomplishment is art work, writing, maps, or work assignments, it is displayed for a week on his bulletin board. What a unique way to validate children!

We could not wait to announce to our group that we were anxious to recognize any student who had made a contribution to school or to fellow students. We set aside an hour or two each Wednesday afternoon for "Student Validation Day." At this time we talk, have refreshments, and hear of all sorts of worthwhile accomplishments of children. Each child is given ten minutes of undivided attention. We then ask our secretary to come in while we dictate a "Good News Letter" to the parents of each child who has received recognition. The letter is then sent in the mail so that a day or two later the parents can also share in the celebration of accomplishment.

An Example of our Good News Letter:

Dear Mrs. Doe,

Recently we started a Student Validation Day honoring students who have made a significant contribution to their school or fellow students. The students receive recognition each Wednesday when they are invited to have cake and talk about their accomplishment.

Your son, Billy, recently undertook a project to decorate our school so it would be more attractive to students. He formed a committee to tape posters and drawings in the hall that would be colorful and interesting to other students. We commend him for this effort and concern. We are proud of Billy and want to share with you how his action has made Boxelder a better school for all of us. Congratulations!

Parents and children alike enjoy these few minutes of affirmation and appreciation because they are direct and related to real situations. Nothing nourishes a person more than honest recognition. Nothing contributes more to a person's being more competent. Oliver Wendell Holmes once wrote, "Man's mind stretched to a new idea never goes back to its original dimensions." We believe!

STRATEGY NO. 6
it's ok to be you

We read the following paragraphs as an introduction to this strategy:
Sometimes one of the most difficult problems we have in the world is being real, being ourselves. It is very important to accept ourselves, for

really, at this very moment, we can't be anything but what we are *now*. Each of us uses up a lot of our energy trying to be something he or she is not:

> We try to appear brave when we are really frightened.
> We try to seem smart when we really don't know.
> We try to be nice when we are really angry.

As long as we continue to bluff our way through life, as long as we pretend, we can never grow. It is only when we say, "I don't know the answer. Can you help me?," or "How can I help myself. What can I do?," that we can really learn something new. In the same way, if we continue to cover up our anger, we can never really feel good or be very good people. Nor can we become brave by pretending. Sometime, someplace it would be great if each of us could say, "I accept myself for what I am," because then and only then can we begin the journey to become something better than we are now.

We continue by introducing the record of Kermit the Frog, "It's Not Easy Being Green." (The version we like is sung by Frank Sinatra in "Frank Sinatra's Greatest Hits," Vol. 2, Reprise Records.) We ask the children to listen closely to the discontented, little green frog's song and see if they can learn the meaning of his words by answering two questions:

1. Why didn't Kermit like being green?
2. What did he discover that made him feel it was OK to be green?

Our children love music so we play records at every opportunity because words set to music hold their interest. If the record is unavailable, you can read this short, paraphrased account of the story:

> *Kermit was a frog.*
> *And if that were not bad enough, he was a rather plain, green frog.*
> *Ugh. How dull!*
> *He spent each day wishing he were RED, or GOLD, just anything except*
> *   EVERY-DAY GREEN.*
> *"Being green, thought Kermit, is really so ordinary. No one ever notices a*
> *   green frog. It would be so much better to be bright and sparkly like*
> *   MOONBEAMS or STAR TWINKLES."*
> *Then he thought a second time,*
> *   "But green is the color of spring, the color of splashing oceans and tall,*
> *   shady trees.*
> *"And what is more,*
> *   green is cool.*
> *   green is friendly.*

green is important."
"Just like me, thought Kermit, green is what I want to be."
And from that time on green-all-over, forever-green Kermit the frog felt
beautiful and fine.

After briefly discussing the two questions, ask: "If you could be any color, what color would you most like to be?" Quickly move around the circle asking for the different color choices. Then group all the children who chose the same color together in small groups. Have each color group stand and quickly validate them with positive qualities those colors represent. (Color projection has become a fascinating area for psychology. See *The Luscher Color Test*, Random House, 1969, and *Color the Real You*, Hemisphere Publications, 1972.)

If the children chose *RED*—these people like action. They have lots of energy. They usually like adventure and variety in their life.

If the children chose *GREEN*—these people tend to be serious and responsible. They try to do the right thing and be fair and honest. They like friends around them who are affectionate.

If the children chose *BLUE*—you like your world to be calm and quiet. You will be calm and sensitive to those around you. You are a very loyal friend.

If the children chose *YELLOW*—those who like yellow are usually artistic. They like new things. They have great imaginations and very deep feelings about life. Usually these people are deep thinkers.

If the children chose *BLACK*—these children probably feel great pressure on their lives and are inclined to be rebellious and dissatisfied. They want very much to gain control of their lives.

If the children chose *PURPLE*—people who prefer purple are usually quite easy to be with. They are sensitive to the needs of others and usually quite tolerant of others. They, too, are inclined to be artistic.

If the children chose *BROWN*—brown is preferred by steady, conscientious people. These people like security. They have a strong sense of duty and can be counted upon to be responsible.

The above basic personality traits are quite general in nature but tend to be consistent in their interpretation. The aim of this exercise is not to be strictly scientific but rather to point out traits that may not have been considered by the children as characteristic of them. In this way they might also gain a new idea of what they are now or what they might become.

The choices of color by our children seemed to be a very valid projective procedure. The most chosen color was brown, which, in general, reflects a need for security and a sense of belonging, along with the above-mentioned positive characteristics. The second most chosen color was purple, which tends to indicate mental and emotional immaturity.

Blue was the third most frequently chosen, reflecting a need for tranquility, peace, relaxation, and rest.

We usually divide this strategy into two sessions as we want to leave the children feeling validated. A second part of the strategy would include asking:

> 1. What is not easy about being you? Shut your eyes and think about this for a moment or two. Then tell us if you feel it is not too personal. We asked for volunteers and the children responded with:

"It's hard being me because I get mad real often."

"It's hard being me cause I get hurt a lot."

"I get mad at people."

"Cause mom and dad are divorced."

"It's hard cause my mom and dad get mad at me."

(The frequency of "mad" (angry) responses clearly points up the need for this group to devote future sessions to anger: when and how to control, sublimate, or discharge it; how to cope with anger in others, etc.)

> 2. What do you like about being you? Close your eyes again and think. Then tell the group why you like being yourself. Some of the responses:

"I get to go on picnics."

"I can have fun with other kids."

"I can draw pictures real good."

"I get to go back to regular school because I've worked."

"I have a good dog."

Frederick Perls spent much of his life in Gestalt Psychology promoting the idea of authenticity—being real! He consistently attacks the idea of pretending. "Most of our whole striving in life is pure fantasy. We don't want to become who we are. We want to become a concept, a fantasy, what we should be like."[9] We want to accept and have our children accept who they are. Authentic people are first of all themselves. They know themselves. They take responsibility for being themselves. Their energy is not dissipated in maintaining a heavy facade or fantasy. They are not "acting like" they are something they are not.

We believe it is most important for our children to be aware and

[9] Perls, Frederick, *Gestalt Therapy Verbatim*, Real People Press, Lafayette, California, 1969, p. 224.

honest about what they experience rather than phoney and denying what they really feel. Carl Rogers wrote about the curious paradox of accepting who and what we are ". . . we cannot change, we cannot move away from what we are, until we thoroughly accept what we are. Then change seems to come about almost unnoticed."[10] We think this strategy promotes children's growth through awareness and acceptance of what is, a discovery from inside.

> 3. As a last part of this strategy, the teachers gave each child personal validation. Perhaps this is a time for us to share a word or two about the language of validation. First of all, validations must be honest. Validations are not meant to be flattering and they are not meant to manipulate children into behavior because that would be an inappropriate use. Validation is clearly "just there" because the children are there and they deserve our looking at their beauty rather than their pimples. Most kids have been thoroughly red-penciled to death. Their parents did an excellent job on them in the beginning by simply calling attention to almost everything that was wrong with them. The language of "red-penciling" is very clear to all of us. It goes like this:

"Chew with your mouth closed"

"Keep your elbows off the table"

"Sit up straight"

"Go upstairs and wash your neck. That is not a shadow. That is dirt"

"Bring your bicycle in. It's going to rust"

"Get those books off the stairs. You want everybody tripping over them?"

The point is that most parents spend an inordinate amount of time red-penciling their children, and in subtle but literal ways they kill those children. And the children need to know that there is also a chance to be validated. Until parents begin to balance the numbers of put-downs and numbers of killer statements, begin to balance them with equal or greater numbers of validation, we are going to raise more and more children who are angry, who are feeling put down, who feel worthless, and whose self-concept is probably about a quarter of an inch tall. So teachers and parents need to learn the language of validation. But it must always be real and must never be manipulative, and above all it must be built into training the children to accept the validation. This means teaching them how to let it in. Here are the sentence stems that teachers and parents need to use, if they're going to begin to practice the language of validation:

"I appreciate you so much for_____."

[10]Rogers, Carl, *On Becoming a Person*, Houghton Mifflin, Boston, 1961, p. 17.

"I need to validate you for_____."

"Let me thank you for_____."

"I love you for_____."

"It makes me so happy when you_____."

There are others, of course, but those are the beginnings of the validation stems and the validation training that grows from these stems.

STRATEGY NO. 7 ————————————————————
lunch box notes

Mr. Charles Schulz, the creator of the "Peanuts" gang, knows with deep insight the world of children and their parents. Some time ago he drew a series of his cartoon strips in which one of the characters, we believe it was Linus, received a daily note from his mother in his lunch bucket. Although our memories regarding the content of those notes have failed us, we nevertheless thought the idea of lunch box notes might be a good way to validate children. One day we asked them to think of the kinds of notes they would like to receive at school in their lunch boxes. These are the messages they would most enjoy:

> Dear son or daughter,
> There will be fresh baked brownies on the cabinet and cold milk in the refrigerator when you get home from school.
> I hope you're having a good day at school today.
> Don't get hurt playing football.
> You may go to the movies after school today with the girls.
> We're proud of the good work you do.
> Yes, you can go fishing after you take out the trash.
>> Love,
>> Mom

We collected the notes and wrote a letter to parents listing those comments that their children appreciated most from them. Then we asked the parents to occasionally write letters to the school that could be opened at noon lunch as a way of validating their children and saying, "We think you're really okay, kid!" These small lunch box tributes have done much to develop the self-esteem of our children.

EIGHT

freedom
to learn

We could cite many educators from John Dewey to John Holt who advocate the element of "personal involvement" in the learning process to insure that the experience is meaningful and significant. For us, Carl Rogers says it so well:

> Let me define a bit more precisely the elements which are experiential learning. It has a quality of personal involvement—the whole person in both his feeling and cognitive aspects being in the learning event. It is self-initiated. Even when the impetus or stimulus comes from the outside, the sense of discovery, of reaching out, of grasping and comprehending, comes from within. It is pervasive. It makes a difference in the behavior, the attitudes, perhaps even the personality of the learner. It is evaluated by the learner. He knows whether it is meeting his need, whether it leads toward what he wants to know, whether it illuminates the dark area of ignorance he is experiencing. The locus of evaluation, we might say, resides definitely in the learner. Its essence is meaning. When such learning takes place, the element of meaning to the learner is built into the whole experience.[1]

In the following eight strategies we have sought to make learning relevant. We have equated learning with discovery. There are many methods of teaching, and we do not purport to be experts in this field. These are simply a few strategies that, we hope, might be helpful:

1. Love and Care (an intimate experience to promote the idea that human beings are capable and lovable)
2. Story Time (an experience in imagination and fantasy)
3. Sharing Circle (gaining closure at the end of each day)
4. Word Jumble
5. Words Are Important (words of relevance from feelings)
6. Kids' Newspaper (gaining self-esteem and achievement through writing)
7. Pet Center (learning from the gentleness of animals)
8. Assimilation (the things we learn)

"What can the schools do to counteract the death wish in kindergarten, to strengthen the wish for life in the first grade?" asked Maslow. Then he answered, "Perhaps the most important thing we can do is to

---

[1] Rogers, Carl R., *Freedom to Learn,* C. E. Merrill, Columbus, Ohio, 1969, p. 5.

give the child a sense of accomplishment."[2] School can be a rewarding place, a place of achievement where self-esteem, self-respect, and high regard for self is nourished.

STRATEGY NO. 1 —————————————————————————————————
love and care

Each morning for fifteen minutes our children gather in small groups of four or five for an intimate experience in love and caring for each other. This is a time to level with children and care for their personal needs. The teachers sit with their small groups on pillows in a circle on the floor to assure eye contact and attentive listening. We refer to this time as "reading the cats," an idea learned from a lion tamer with the circus who said that as his lions and tigers bounded from their cages down the long shoot to the central arena, he had just thirty seconds to determine the mood of each particular animal. He then based his entire performance on how each individual animal felt. The trainer had learned the importance of considering the feelings of his animals.

It is during love and caring time that we "read the kids" and take into account their moods and feelings. During this short session we might learn that one child did not sleep well, another missed breakfast, one was yelled at because his jeans were torn, another has a headache. These are all potential blocks to learning and must be cleared or discharged. This can be done by talking about it, which is often enough if someone is there to really listen. We use other forms of caring appropriate to the occasion: massage, relaxation, holding, feeding, free time, etc.

In Sid's little booklet, *I Am Loveable and Capable* (Argus Communications, Niles, Illinois, 1973), he writes about the invisible signs each of us wear with the initials *IALAC*, standing for "I am loveable and capable." The point of this simple yet profound booklet is that "people need to understand and care about one another." "Love and Care Time" is a practical application of that principle.

---

[2]Maslow, Abraham H., *The Farther Reaches of Human Nature,* Viking Press, Inc., New York, 1971, p. 188.

STRATEGY NO. 2 ——————————————————————
story time

Here and now experiences are so necessary to health. They enable us to relax, to listen, to see, and be fully a part of something. Our story time proves the point that learning can come easy in an atmosphere of enjoyment and fun. When the children gather around their teacher for a story, they learn many things: the pleasure of good literature, values others hold, how to listen, and how to communicate an idea.

We remember reading a piece of research indicating that children in the Scandinavian countries read better than children from other European countries because, for one thing, they have been read to by their fathers. Therefore, we hold that story time is a prerequisite for a child learning to read and for building a vocabulary of words with meaning.

But primarily story time is a break for children at mid-morning, and while the teachers drink tea or coffee, the children sip fruit juice and eat cookies and journey to worlds beyond.

After the story we provide opportunities for journeys into daydreaming and fantasy.

Daydreaming. We ask the children to relax, close their eyes, remember the story they have just heard, really become absorbed in the experience and become a part of it. From there they allow their thoughts to wander to other ideas and events if they choose, but mainly they just allow thoughts to happen. Three or four minutes of this experiencing relieves a lot of tension. We usually ask the children to begin with four and count backwards to zero and at that time open their eyes. We suggest they will feel calm, quiet, and relaxed.

Fantasy. At the conclusion of certain stories we guide a child into a fantasy experience. If the story were about a bird, for example, we play soft background music and have the children "soar into the limitless sky—dive down, down, down, down through layers of puffy white clouds—feel warm sunshine—the cool cloud mist—make sweeping circles in the sky, see the world below, float, float, float."

Fantasy nourishes the imagination, stimulates good feelings, fosters creativity, provides hope. Einstein, the great thinker, once said, "Imagination is more important than knowledge."

STRATEGY NO. 3 ─────────────────────
sharing circle

As each school day nears completion we gather the children into small groups once again for a wrapup session to share the day's activities. Closure, as we have stated before, is an important idea. It is best to finish situations and not carry over old tensions, resentments, and frustrations into new activities. They will tend to color our participation and involvement. Paradoxically, one method we use to "finish" the day is with "unfinished" sentences. We ask children to close their eyes, think through their day and begin a sentence or two with:

"I wish _____."

"I learned _____."

"I wonder _____."

"I enjoyed _____."

"I felt good when _____."

"I don't like _____."

"If only _____."

"I would change _____."

Many times this strategy will stimulate ideas for closure through discussion and action.

We have found this is also a good time to send "I urge" telegrams in which students and teachers alike convey something of importance to another person.

Our sharing session sometimes ends with simple "asking." Students are encouraged to ask members of the group or teachers for what they desire. It is an important concept for children to learn to ask for what they need and to discover for themselves that in most instances people are capable and willing to respond to their needs.

STRATEGY NO. 4 ─────────────────────
word jumble

One way we encourage creativity in writing for our more advanced students is to have them pick two or three words from a box and then write a story suggested by the words. Into the box go words like "ghost," "balloons," "horses," "ate," "ran," "fly," "sing," and "laugh" (only nouns and verbs are included).

One of our sixth grade boys drew from the box "balloons," "ghost," and "ate." From this unlikely combination he wrote the following story.

The Ghost Who Ate Balloons

Once upon a time there was a ghost that ate balloons. That was all he ate, and he loved it! As a matter of fact, he made his own balloons for dinner. But one day he started to blow up, higher and higher. He didn't know what to do. Two hours later he was 100 feet tall! He couldn't pop. But all of a sudden he was turning visible. Even worse, all different colors from the colored balloons! He couldn't get any help because there weren't any ghosts in his area. But then the other ghosts from far away sensed something was wrong with their friend ghost through private sensors that ghosts had. They came sweeping to the rescue, but they didn't know what to do either. But then one of them thought of an idea. It was: all the other ghosts would take him to the ocean and throw him in. Then he wouldn't want to drown so he would blow out all the air in him, and he would go back to the same size again. And it worked, but he couldn't get to his normal color again, and he never did. He is still the same colored ghost. Now all the other ghosts call him Colorama.

by Dave

A younger child, who could not read, drew one word, "horse." He was told his word was horse. After some thought he dictated his story.

A Horse

The white horse ran away.
He was not behind the barn.
He was not in front of the barn.
He was far into the woods.
A bear scared the horse,
And the horse came back.

by Jimmy

The children are always happy with their work and we always show how much we value their achievement by including each one in our school newspaper.

STRATEGY NO. 5 ——————————————————————————
words are important

All of us who have read the delightful book, *Teacher*, have been impressed with the approach of Sylvia Ashton-Warner in teaching children to read. She begins by asking each child what word he or she wants most to learn. The words the child chooses are from his or her own world and bound up with personal emotions of hope and fear. The teacher prints each child's word on a card and allows the child to hold it and become acquainted with the word. It is then placed in a pile with other children's words and they see if they can retrieve it. With this as a beginning it is only a short step to having the children write their own word.

We gave each child two 3 × 5 cards and asked them to sit quietly by themselves, close their eyes, and think of two words they would really like to know how to read. After a moment or two of thought, each child went to the teacher and had each word printed on their cards in bold felt-pen letters. The children then studied their words, and when they were ready, told the group why their words were important to them personally. After sharing their words with the group and engaging in a short discussion of them, they placed their word cards in the center of the circle on the floor. Each child in turn repeated this sequence until there was a pile of words scattered in the center of the group. The words were thoroughly mixed like a deck of cards and each child was asked to retrieve his or her word and hold it up. All of our children were able to accurately pick out their words so it was a time for celebration and validation for the success of each child.

Our children chose significant words from their own personal world:

Throat and Tonsils: Chosen by a girl whose brother was to undergo a tonsillectomy. "The *tonsils* are in his *throat*," she said. "I wanted to know about them."

Semi-truck and Trumpeter Swan: By a boy who wants to be a semi-truck driver "when I'm older" and would "sure like to see a trumpeter swan."

Dad and Sister: Words important to one of our younger children who could not explain why she chose these particular words. We felt they were significant because she has recently lost her "Dad" through divorce and longs to see him. She also plays Cinderella to an older "sister" whom the mother prefers.

Life and Pervert: "The kids in the neighborhood call me 'pervert.' I'd like to know what it means." (We discussed this.) "I just think the word 'Life' is important. It's important to have a happy life."

Operation and Die: "I guess you all know my mother has had a lot of 'Operations' and I worry about her 'Dying."

Snow and Monster: "I like to play in the 'Snow' and I like to watch 'Monster' movies on TV."

Horse and Car: Chosen by a boy who could not express reasons for his choice. We know he loves "Horses" but could not accurately understand his reason for "Car." He has been regarded as a nonreader but he certainly knew these words.

Troubles and Clothes: "Troubles is my dog and I like nice 'Clothes.' "

Joe and Easter Bunny: By another "nonreader" who has an older brother named 'Joe' and who "likes the 'Easter Bunny.' "

Operation and Frankenstein: Strange that this boy chose words similar to two other children but it was coincidental because he had no way of knowing their words since he was not with the same teacher. "Operation because my mom has had quite a few" and "Frankenstein because he's scarey."

All words are powerful abstracts of life. Words, especially those chosen by children like "semi-truck," "operation," and "pervert" carry with them great impact, worth, and meaning. These most important words to children are not always dignified as with ghetto children who prefer to learn the four letter variety. But make no mistake about this—words always emerge out of life, always they are connected-to-life, a part of a child's world, a part of the child's value system, and as such they are value-able to know.

Followup Activity

The next day each child drew a picture on the back of each card to illustrate the two words. These were then used as flash cards showing first the word and if the child could not remember it, the drawing served as a visual reminder. If this is done daily, a child soon builds a large vocabulary of words and the number of cards serve as a reinforcement to learning—a validation of achievement!

STRATEGY NO. 6 ——————————————————
kids' newspaper

Twice each month our school publishes a mimeographed newspaper, "Boxelder News." Once a week the teachers interview our reporters (all the children in the school) to learn if they have art work, stories, or announcements to make. A newspaper box is also provided for newsworthy ideas. The general format of the "News" is to give recognition and validation to the students. Some examples of our general headlines and captions are as follows:

Hello

Joe Doe and Mary Smith are two kids who started school at Boxelder this month. It's sure good to have you both here.

Thank You

John's mom, for sending us cookies. Toby and John for cleaning up the storeroom without being asked.

Did You Know?

Patty has started ballet lessons and finished VAD Book I this week.

Jack has learned a new cheer: Two bits, four bits, six bits, a dollar. All for Boxelder, stand up and holler.

Writer's Corner

(In this column children write about meaningful experiences.) "Mary went away to a special school last year. Today she came back to visit. She was quiet and happy. She stepped in the door and surprised me, I jumped halfway out of my seat. Gosh, did I ever! I was reading my book when she came in and gave me a good one.

by George

Wanted

Left over seeds and potting soil.
Scraps of wood for wood projects.

Did You Know?

Jim has learned to play checkers.

Patrice has started art groups in the afternoon so every student has a special "art day" each week.

Rumors

There's talk about fixing up the Club House. Anyone with ideas about ways to do this can put them in the newspaper box for publication next time or bring them up at our next group meeting.

Recognition

Jim and Brad can now count and write to 100.

Bobby, for putting up posters in the hall and thinking up the idea to use rubber tires and ropes as swings.

Important Dates

March 12—Bookmobile

March 17—Al's birthday

March 19–21—Spring Vacation

I Wish

I wish I had one hundred rabbits.

I wish I was six foot six.

I wish I was the best reader in the whole school.

The Neatest Thing that Has Happened Lately

My birthday!

I got my bike fixed.

My dad gave me a valentine.

Letters

(Occasionally we receive letters from former students, parents, friends, and visitors of interest to our children.)

Quiz

What are the names of our bus drivers?

What's special about next Friday? (Answers will appear next week.)

I'd Like To Be

A dog—I'd bark a lot.

A horse—to run and buck.

A piano—so I could make music.

What We Learned This Week

To build with wood better.

To count money.

To talk in groups.

To get along with kids.

Field Trips

Don't forget to pack your own lunch for a trip to the fire station this Friday.

In two weeks we plan to go to the Rock Fort.

Goodbye

Toby is going back to regular school. We'll miss you, Toby.

Our interns will leave next week, too. Good luck!

STRATEGY NO. 7 —————————————————————
the pet center

Early in the school year we were casually talking with some of the children and asked them, "What is important—really? What are the important things in life?" (We later formalized this into a strategy we called "Brainstorming Life's Values," which is covered on page 56.) They thought awhile and then listed some of their priorities.

Food is important.

Pets are important.

At staff meeting we discussed how we might implement in our program the importance kids give to food and pets.

As for food we decided to cook our own lunches instead of having them catered. We had a stove, a refrigerator, and odds and ends of utensils. As a result the children now help plan the menus, shop for the food, prepare and serve it, and clean up afterwards. They feel real pride and accomplishment from working in "their" kitchen.

The idea of pets intrigued us too. Already there was an independent yellow cat that wandered aimlessly through the school at his own discretion and the children loved him. One of the authors had read about delinquent children being assigned pets to care for and how this had resulted in an empathy for animals that extended or transferred to people. So we asked the children to bring any pets they would like to have at school. We did specify that the animals would have to be content to stay in one room called a pet center. This excluded dogs, cats, and other larger animals. In a few weeks we had snakes, a guinea pig, craw-dads, insects of all kinds, fish, and gerbils—all lovingly brought from home with the parents' happy consent. The children take turns caring for the animals and playing with them and experiencing to some degree what Walt Whitman felt when he wrote ". . . I think I could turn and live with animals, they are so placid and self-contained; I stand and look at them long and long."

THE FINAL STRATEGY ———————————
assimilation

In this small book we held to the idea that it is not necessary to *force* or *make* children grow. We simply sought to provide some *help* along the way with opportunities for them to choose their alternatives, feel some pride in the choices they made and then act upon their convictions so that there was less confusion and more understanding in their lives.

At our final group meeting we asked the children, for the last time, to close their eyes, reflect back over the entire year of schooling, and highpoint one or two things they had learned at Boxelder. We asked them, as we had on so many other occasions, to begin their sentences with, "I learned _____ ." They took stock and answered:

I learned not to destroy things

to get along with teachers better

to divide by two numbers

to help with the kitchen and cook

to behave better

to read library books

to do stuff with wood and make things

to count money

to play kickball

to talk in a group

to do exercises

to type letters

to get outside faster at recess

I learned a lot about firetrucks.

We have come to believe that for most people growth comes slowly, not in great gobs of insight, not suddenly and dramatically. Growth is a gentle unfolding, and these children, we think, have made a start in that direction of healthy becoming. They have started to "search for" and form values but equally important they have begun to value themselves as human beings capable of learning and loving. Maslow said it best when he wrote, "Indeed I think it possible that we may soon even DE-FINE therapy as a *search* for values, because ultimately the *search* for identity, is in essence, the *search* for one's own intrinsic, authentic values."[3]

---

[3]Maslow, Abraham, H., *Toward a Psychology of Being,* Van Nostrand Reinhold, New York, 1968, p. 177.

NINE

parent involvement

---

dinner table learning
and prescriptions for parents

Throughout the school year conferences are held with the Boxelder parents to explain how they can work with the school in meeting the needs of their children. We never ask parents to tutor their children in academic areas, rather we assign them tasks in the form of dinner table learning and prescriptions which underscore the relevance of self-actualization. In these ways we hope to encourage personal growth as well as family integration.

As parents aid us, we ask them to be themselves, real people not amateur psychologists, and not teachers, because these are facades that destroy the relationship so important to learning. Children do not like pretense. They learn best in relationship with ". . . a vital person, with convictions, with feelings."[1]

Children learn best when their feelings and opinions are accepted and prized. This means sometimes accepting occasional apathy on the part of the learner. It means understanding feelings even when they tend to disturb the parent. It implies trust and caring in spite of differences.

Rogers feels a third important element in the learning process is "empathetic understanding" for the learner, ". . . to understand the student's reactions from the inside,"[2] to be sensitive to how it seems to the student. These qualities promote learning and are attitudes we suggest parents experiment with as they work with their children in the home, around the dinner table, on walks, and in casual conversation.

DINNER TABLE LEARNING
AND PRESCRIPTIONS FOR PARENTS

Most schools seek, in many ways, to elicit parental support and involvement with education. Parental investment of time and interest both enhances and accelerates the whole process of learning as well as therapy. We have devised two strategies—Dinner Table Learning and Prescriptions—designed to extend the school program into the home in meaningful, simple, and fun ways. By following these methods parents discover many aspects of themselves as well as their children.

[1]Rogers, Carl R., *Freedom to Learn*, Charles E. Merrill, Columbus, Ohio, 1969, p. 107.
[2]Ibid., p. 111.

Dinner table learning is a strategy for making the family dinner table a learning center, a place and time where discovery, amazement, and wonder are shared in an informal, open-ended way. Usually our teachers will ask the parents to set one evening aside for dinner table learning through discussion. Another evening in the week is set aside for prescriptions, a more action-centered approach. In combination, these two strategies encompass the process of valuing which is *choosing* and *prizing* values through discussion and *acting* upon these values in a consistent pattern of living.

Forty Dinner Table Strategies[3]

1. Invite each person around the table to discuss "the high point of my day" or if a member did not experience a "lift," tell "How it feels not to have a high point." (Of course in all of these discussions a member is always given the option to "pass" if he or she chooses. Discussion should always be voluntary rather than forced. Unnecessary moralizing is also not recommended because children soon "turn off" to this familiar style of indoctrination.)
2. Each family member takes a turn to discuss "something new I have learned today and how this knowledge will help me live life a little more fully." (Always encourage brief statements. These conversations are not intended to be exhaustive. The whole process on any given evening should not take more than twenty minutes. If the discussion continues to motivate and excite, time limits may be extended.)
3. Talk about a "kindness shown to me today or a kindness I was able to give to someone else."
4. Ask each person to name one family strength he or she feels is important. Examples: We always take a vacation together. We don't yell at each other. We have fun together at the football game.
5. Discuss: "Three things I love about our family."
6. For a moment each member of the family thinks about the clothes he or she wore that day, and they explain what they wanted their clothes to say about them.
7. Talk for a few minutes about "what each person would like to change about their life" and "what prevents them from changing."
8. Members of a family need to share the concerns and problems of each other occasionally, so for one topic discuss "The lowest point in my life last week."
9. Think about some "things you would like to do better" and take turns discussing these.
10. Try an exercise in active listening. The first person to participate writes a sentence so it is preserved accurately. That person then repeats the sentence to the person on his right. This is repeated until the last person is reached. The accuracy of the message is then checked against the written sentence. The family then considers how attentively they feel they listen to each other.

[3]For additional suggestions see our appendix "Dinner Table Learning."

11. Ask each person at the dinner table to name three things they think they are "good at doing."

12. Each person is asked to give one motto, saying, or sentence that he or she tries to live by. Enhance the experience by holding hands around the table.

13. Discuss one piece of "unfinished business" each member of the family has left over. "Unfinished business" is a term for something not completed, something that is still "left hanging" or "up in the air." Unfinished business usually clamors for completion and until the business is "finished," there is usually a feeling of uneasiness or tension.

14. A good theme for discussion is "the best teacher I ever had" and "the most valuable lesson I learned from this teacher."

15. Each member, in turn, faces the other members of the family and asks each one individually, "What can I do to help you?"

16. For a light topic for conversation consider "the funniest thing that happened to me last week."

17. For a more serious consideration: "How I would change the world if I had the influence to do so."

18. Each member of the family is asked: "If you were a tree, what kind of tree would you be?" or "If you were a vegetable or fruit or car what kind would you be?" Another slightly different way to phrase the theme for discussion is to fill in these blanks: "Today I feel like a (name a tree, vegetable, car) because

19. After a week's search of the newspaper, each person brings an interesting topic to discuss.

20. Tell the funniest joke or story you have heard this past week.

21. Discuss: Ways to beautify our home.
    Ways to settle family arguments.
    Ways to have more joy.

22. Consider: What traditions or rituals do we observe as a family? How did these come to be? Are they important?

23. Tell about an important "turning point" in your life.

24. Each member of the family makes up three sentences beginning with the words, "I wonder   "

25. For another "news" discussion ask the question, "What recent piece of news disturbed you the most lately? What other piece gave you hope?"

26. Family names always have much personal meaning. Ask each person to talk about or question parents regarding: What my name means? How I received my name? My nicknames and how I got these names. A name I would prefer to be called.

27. Think about decisions: "An important decision I made today." "An important decision I wish I had made." "An important decision I hope to make." "Why I am delaying certain decisions."

28. The "good times" are important to recall and affirm from time to time, so consider the question, "When do I really enjoy being alive?"

29. "Shoulds" and "oughts" need examination from time to time. Ask each person to "name three things I should or ought to do. Who says I should? What would I prefer?"

30. Tell the other members of the family what your favorite toy is.
31. If each member of the family was an animal what would they be. Focus on one member of the family at a time and begin a sentence such as "Dad would be a _____because_____."
After each person gives an idea of what kind of animal they feel Dad is most like, he is asked to tell what kind of animal he would most like to be and why?
32. For a quick "turn around the table" ask each person, "Who do you admire most in public life and why?"
33. Spiritual things: How does the family or each of us receive inspiration, hope, beliefs, values? Are there other ways to in-spirit us and guard us against despair? What are "ways" others find to be life-validating?
34. Simple questions: Each person chooses one to answer.
Would you prefer to be younger or older in age than you are now?
Are most kids happy?
Do you ever wish you were someone different—Who?
Will you ever grow a beard and let your hair grow long? Why?
What was your best year?
Are you a rebel or conformist?
What do you prize most?
Are you curious about trying pot, smoking, alcohol?
What was your favorite movie—your favorite movie star?
What's the scariest thing that ever happened to you?
What's your favorite place on earth?
What do you need most?
How do you cope with anger?
How do you handle sadness?
When did you come closest to dying?
Can you ever recall stealing anything?
How would you improve your life?
What would you do with $500.00?
Will you ever get married?
How many children would you like to have?
What vocation would you choose?
Do you believe in God? Do you believe in reincarnation or heaven? What happens after death?
What is your favorite book?
What is best/worst about school?
Who do you dislike most?
What is your stand on birth control pills?
What do you admire most in people?
What have you stood up for recently?
What do you worry about?
35. Rank ordering is an exercise in making choices between competing alternatives. A few suggestions are given as examples for possible dinner table conversation.
Where would you rather live—in the city? in the country? by the sea? in the mountains?
Do you learn best by listening? By reading? By discussing?
Who would you rather be—a Mexican-American, an American Negro? an Anglo-American?

What is your favorite time of year? Summer—Spring—Fall—Winter?
Which is most harmful in your opinion—Pot—Alcohol—Cigarettes?

36. On a designated children's night parents are asked to say, from the
    heart, five good things about each of their children. At another time
    children reciprocate by enumerating five good things about their par-
    ents.

37. Have one evening in which each member of the family can express
    one of the following:

I need

I want

I would like

Then determine how the family can help meet these expressed needs.

38. Ask each member to state "something I wanted to happen today" and
    tell whether it did happen and how. If the "wanting" was unfulfilled
    tell why and how you felt about it.

39. Set aside three minutes of uninterrupted time in which each member
    of the family may talk about anything he or she desires. To talk with-
    out interruption and have the feeling that people are there for you,
    listening, is a rare and refreshing experience.

40. Each person is asked to discuss the most exciting, frightening, depress-
    ing, boring, fatiguing, angry, happy, loving thing that happened in
    "my life today."

These forty strategies are intended only as "seed" to give the flavor
and style of discussion. Teachers and families themselves soon learn to
discuss topics relevant to them.

Occasionally our teachers set aside class time after a family discussion evening and ask a few children to share their experience so the whole
class can learn about other families, beliefs, thoughts, and values. Never
is a child asked to violate a family confidence and no family is ever "put
down" for what they choose to believe.

In our strategy, "Family Prescriptions" an actual prescription form
is sent home.

FAMILY PRESCRIPTION FORM

Rx:
  What to do:

  How to do it:

  When to do it:

  How often:

A simple example is:

What to do: Hug each other.

How to do it: Gently and with love.

When to do it: Anytime but most often when leaving or returning from work or school and in the evening before supper and bedtime.

How often: A minimum of three times per day in order to overcome skin hunger and insure love. Continue each day for maximum results.

We have adapted the following thirty-one suggestions for Rx cards:

1. Read your child a bedtime story at least once a week. Make this a special time with cookies and milk.
   To learn about your child's favorite stories, ask him or her to help you make a list. If these are not available at home, ask the teacher or city librarian to help you obtain copies.
2. Plan an "evening out" with your child by asking what would be the most "fun" thing to do. Most children enjoy simple events such as going for a hamburger or pizza, taking a walk, going to a movie, eating ice cream, playing a game, taking in a sports event, a ride in the car, or a visit with someone or to some place.
3. At bedtime give your child a soothing massage or a tension-reducing back scratch along with a kiss.
4. For one day ask each person to be a "good deeds detective" and keep account of all the good things he or she observed taking place during the day. Report on these events at the dinner table.
5. Experience a silent meal in which no one talks. The focus is to sensitively sense the need of each other and quietly respond to it. Examples: Little sister may need a napkin. Someone becomes aware of her need and gives her one. Dad has eaten his potatoes and may want a second helping. Someone responds. Mother will need help cleaning the table after the meal, etc. All members are asked to respond nonverbally to others' needs.
6. For one week each member of the family has a "secret pal" whose name is drawn from a hat. The secret pals then practice caring and loving acts toward each other in the family for one week. On the final day members of the family try to guess their secret pals and thank them for their acts of kindness and love.
7. Each member of the family chooses a favorite record and plays it; afterwards explaining why the particular selection was chosen.
8. Several weeks in advance of the event, make plans how a traditional holiday can become more meaningful and worthwhile for the family.
9. Separately, at first, draw a family coat of arms including:

   Each member submits his or her ideas and these are condensed into a final coat of arms that characterizes the family, their ideals, beliefs, values, and accomplishments.

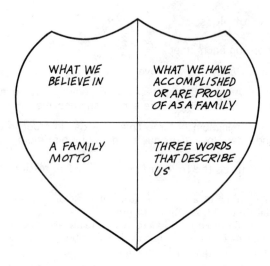

10. Draw a life line from birth to death. Locate with an "X" where you believe yourself to be now. Then discuss three things you would like to accomplish in the next ten years.

11. As a family write a letter of concern to an editor, a congressional representative, an administrator and sign it as a family. Later discuss the response you did or did not receive.

12. Most cities or towns encourage citizens to become better acquainted with the police and their work in the community. One of their methods of informing the public is to invite citizens to ride in a patrol car for a few hours. If this is possible in your town arrange for members of the family to do this and then discuss the experience.

13. "Sentence stems" or "unfinished sentences" hold potential for gaining insight into family dynamics. Jot off three or four "stems" to discuss on different occasions:

Dad always _____ .

Mother is _____ .

Sister seems _____ .

Brother thinks _____ .

I am happy when _____ .

I need _____ .

I get angry when _____ .

I believe _____ .

Others hurt my feelings by _____ .

My best days are _____ .

I'm afraid _____ .

It makes me sad when _____ .

My family is _____ .

I wish we _____ .

We need more time _____ .

I need more time _____ .

14. Things to do in the kitchen:
Bake a cake or cookies with your child
Carve a pumpkin
Pop popcorn
Fix a hot or cold drink depending on the season
Sing "round" songs together as you "do" the dishes
Clean out drawers
Divide up to sweep, clean, wax, polish the floor
Make carmel apples
Toast marshmallows

15. Turn off the TV for one evening. The next evening talk about how each member "spent" the evening and how they felt about being without TV.

16. Plan a new family holiday. Give it a name. Decide *when* it will be celebrated, *why* it will be celebrated, and *how*.

17. Before dinner ask each member of the family to draw themselves as a tree. How would they portray themselves as trees?

18. Thoughtful action—consider, "What one thing, if changed, would improve our town? What can we do about it?" When will we take action?

19. Take a quiet, nonverbal walk together and experience things through the five senses: feeling, smelling, looking, tasting, listening. After returning home share the experience together.

20. Prepare warm bubble baths for each other and where appropriate bathe together.

21. Initiate a "People Appreciation Night" on one evening. Ask the parents to say, from the heart, five things they appreciate about their children. On an alternate evening the children give five appreciations to their parents.

22. Most of us are not "touched" enough and so we suffer from "skin hunger." To overcome this deficiency we suggest "hug days" for a prescription. Each member of the family should make it a point to hug every other member a minimum of four times per day. Suggested hug times: Before leaving for work or school, upon return from work or school, before dinner, once in the evening, and always prior to bed time.

23. Choose a clear day on the weekend and watch the clouds forming in the sky. Make up fantasies of what the clouds represent.

24. Plan a picnic, or go to the zoo, the museum, the library to choose a book to read together as a family. Is there a park in town with a lake

and ducks to feed? What about a ride in the country? A walk along a
nature trail?

25. Choose a few games to play together: cards, checkers, monopoly,
    bingo, etc.

26. On a large strip of paper (most schools would be happy to supply you
    with this) together draw your family "doing something." Discuss what
    you learned from the experience.

27. Draw names and buy a plant for each member of the family to care
    for.

28. Dig out all the old family photograph albums and talk about the family
    history with all its characters.

29. Together rearrange a room so it is more comfortable to live in.

30. On successive evenings have one or two people in the family plan,
    cook, and serve the evening meal. All those who are not on the plan-
    ning, cooking, or serving, must clean up and wash the dishes.

31. Share a childhood memory. This is especially interesting if parents can
    share memories from their own childhood relative to the present age
    of their children. Children are simply asked to share any memory over
    a year old.

appendix

In this appendix we have included four articles which help give added meaning to the preceding pages.

The first, "Programming for Troubled Children," gives an overview of the daily program at Boxelder School. The second, "Dinner Table Learning," explains further the use of this strategy along with additional specific suggestions for implementation. The third, "How Sixty Teachers Learned to Think Like Children Once Again," are ideas from a workshop that could be used with faculties for inservice training. The last article, "Getting to Know You," outlines four strategies designed to bring students and teachers closer together in authentic relationship.

Grateful acknowledgement is given for permission to reprint the following articles.

PROGRAMMING FOR TROUBLED CHILDREN ————

"How terrible to see the light go out of a child's eyes, to feel defensive stiffness growing in hunched little shoulders, sensing mistrust and calculated distance being woven into the fabric of a fresh new life."[1]

This year we[2] were given the opportunity to bring the excitement back into the eyes of sixteen elementary age, severely emotionally disturbed children . . . to teach them trust and, we hope, reduce their loneliness. We knew from the beginning we must have empathy for "failures" since this was the label that was seared into these students' psyche by the regular classrooms. It was tragic enough that others had rejected them but even more depressing that even they had introjected the verdict and misguided diagnosis, thus regarding themselves as "dumb, stupid, and bad." Our program of intervention was designed to nourish hope and surprise these children with new concepts of what they might become!

      9:00– 9:15—Love and Care
      9:15– 9:30—Body Awakening
      9:30–10:00—Story Time
   10:00–10:20—Free Play

[1]McMahon, Edwin M. and Peter A. Campbell, *Please Touch*, Sheed & Ward, New York, 1969, p. 8.
[2]Nancy Burgess and Al Kuehnast, teachers; Bob O'Rourke, Psychologist.

10:20–11:20—Headtripping
11:20–11:30—Please Touch
11:30–12:30—Lunch and Recess
12:30– 2:00—Projects
 2:00– 2:15—Sharing Time
 2:20–   —Going Home (our children were on a modified day schedule.)

At the beginning we were fortunate enough to be given two gifts that helped us build a program that had a good prognosis for developing successful learning experiences for children: 1. Two capable, loving teachers who felt good about themselves as human beings. (Only such as these can reach out and tenderly touch the soul of a troubled child.) 2. Unlimited freedom to design innovative programs for children. In this article we share our program in hope that it might possess useful adaptations for both the regular and special classroom.

We begin each day with "Love and Care," an intimate experience between the children and their teacher. The children have informally designed their love and care "centers" with pillows, posters, and rugs in secluded corners of the room, conducive to talk. Talking is one of the better ways we know of to heal the hurt of our children. The children are encouraged to talk about "NOW" situations in their lives—fear of separation and divorce—the bully who taunts them at the bus stop—the cat that ran away. The talk is not always negative, although it is spontaneous. There are times of celebration—the new baby sister—a weekend fishing trip—a funny picture show. It is rare that these children are afforded unconditional listening without interruption and with affirmation. We teach the children to ask for what they need at these times because they are assured this is a concerned group that loves and cares and can respond to their needs.

Having honored the feelings of each child, we now wake up their bodies with rolling, tumbling on mats, hitting the punching bag, swinging, and in many and various ways exercising and coordinating the large muscle systems of their bodies in physical release and tension reduction. "When the body activities are successful, they lead to a feeling of more freedom and an increase in the concept of the self as a capable person, both essential ingredients of joy."[3]

After body awareness-release, we gather by interest and age groups for "Story Time." Stories are chosen by the children for the most part to insure interest while fruit juice and graham crackers are served to enhance the enjoyment of the experience. In this relaxed, easy atmos-

---

[3]Schutz, William C., *Joy, Expanding Human Awareness*, Grove Press, New York, 1967, p. 50.

phere, vocabulary and motivation for reading is developed while children learn to listen and respond.

There is always time to daydream a while and reflect back over the theme of the story and how it affects the children's personal lives. Sometimes we guide the children on a fantasy trip or ask them to create and write a story of their own. This story time becomes an adventure and springboard to many intuitive, creative activities as well as a stimulation of imagination, which Einstein regarded as " . . . more important than knowledge."

Throughout the day we attempt to pace our program to the physical-emotional needs of children: quiet times, active times, thoughtful-reflective times, moving-action times. We regard free play, our next scheduled activity, as a transition period between story time and headtripping.

The children chose "headtripping" as their name for reading and arithmetic. Half of the group are seen for individual prescriptive teaching in arithmetic while the other half are seen for reading. At the end of thirty minutes, the two groups rotate. Each child is given immediate feedback on his or her successes as well as mistakes (the latter is minimized). We do not "red-pencil" these children; we tell them mistakes help them learn also. Trial and error is still a valid method that most of us use outside the classroom in real-life situations. If these children can learn to accept mistakes as human, they can use them as stepping stones to success. Any child who spells "apple," "appel" is not totally wrong, in fact this child is $4/5$ correct!

Just prior to lunch the mats are pulled out, a quiet record spins a soothing song, and we relax with touch and massage. In these few therapeutic moments we take turns rubbing shoulders, scratching backs, pressing, kneading, stroking. For many of our children we are reaching back to the first year of life to supply the need for touch they were deprived of then. Harvey Jakins has written that each human being needs four hugs a day to survive. Our skins were made for touching in tender, caring, friendly ways. Such touching is always therapeutic!

After lunch and recess our schedule calls for a variety of twenty-minute time periods given to art, films, woodwork, music, health talks, spelling, and writing for the school newspaper. These less demanding cognitive projects are reserved for the afternoon when children are less motivated to learn.

Our day closes as it begins with an intimate, small group of children sharing their day's experiences. We have found this an opportune time to use many of the techniques suggested by Values Clarification. We ask the children to close their eyes, think back through their day and begin a sentence with:

I wish _____ .

I learned _____ .

I wonder _____ .

I enjoyed _____ .

I felt good when _____ .

If only _____ .

I don't like _____ .

I would change _____ .

We have also found this is a good time to send "I Urge Telegrams" in which students and teachers alike convey something of importance to another person.

Charles Schulz, in his comic strip "Peanuts," draws the little girl "with naturally curly hair" seated at her desk struggling with the topic, "What I learned in school this year." After biting her pencil in thoughtful contemplation, she writes, "This year I learned to keep an eye on my lunch so it doesn't get ripped off!"

We felt that "What I learned in school this year" might be very appropriate as a last general group session with our children. We asked them to begin one or two sentences with, "I learned _____ ." They took stock and answered:

Not to destroy things.
To get along with teachers better.
To divide by two numbers.
I learned to behave.
To help in the kitchen and cook.
To read better.
To count money.
To do stuff with wood.
To get along with kids.
To read library books.
To do exercises and play kickball.
To talk in a group.
To type letters.
To get outside faster at recess.
I learned about firetrucks.

For us these responses helped validate our efforts and work for the year. We were grateful that our children did not report facts alone because most of these are forgotten very quickly. The important thing to us was that they had come to know themselves a little better.

DINNER TABLE LEARNING⁴ ────────────────────

What would happen at your dinner table if each member of the family were asked to draw his version of a Family Coat of Arms? Supply each person with a shield-like design divided into six sections, like this:

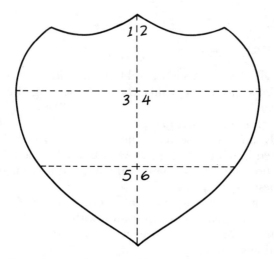

Children and parents can draw a simple sketch in each section. Use words only in section six. No awards will be given for art. The focus is upon values issues represented by each picture and what they say about what this family values.

1. In the first section, draw a picture which represents your view of your family's greatest achievement.
2. To the right of the first section, draw pictures to represent two things *you* are good at. Any two things.
3. Draw a picture showing your greatest failure in the past year.
4. Make a drawing symbolizing one issue, one value, about which you would never budge. It is one of *your* deepest commitments.
5. In the fifth section, draw a picture representing something you are striving to obtain. (It can be material goods, a personality trait, or an abstraction, etc.)
6. This is the only block on which to write words. Pick three words which you think should become the family motto. They can be three separate words or three words which make a sentence. They should be three words the whole family could believe in.

⁴Simon, Sidney B., "Dinner Table Learning," *Colloquy*, Dec. 1971. Used by permission.

Each member then shares his coat of arms, one at a time, explaining why he drew what he drew. The discussion should help to clarify and strengthen certain ideas which will ultimately appear in the Family Coat of Arms—the six blocks representing a consensus of all the family members. The final task is to divide up the six blocks, with each member being responsible for at least one block, some doing two or more. Again, art is not the important idea. Values are. The final product is a group-built Family Coat of Arms.

Rank Orders

An easy but important and ongoing exercise to liven up the dinner table, and one which gets children and parents alike to look at moral decisions, I call Rank Orders.

Members of the family are given three items. Each person is asked to state his personal preferences. Here are some examples:

Which is the stupidest thing to do of these three?

a. To drive a car after an ice storm and scrape a hole only the size of a half-dollar to see through.
b. Always to ride a motorcycle without a helmet.
c. To start smoking cigarettes as a teenager.

Let me stress that there is no right answer to this Rank Order. Each person sees it from his own perspective. If the family can resist the easy temptation to moralize over a "right answer," a lot of searching and inquiring into each person's values can take place. And the search is fun and lively.

Another example:

Which would be the best job for you of these three?

a. To be a pickle inspector in a pickle factory, eight hours a day pulling damaged pickles off the conveyer belt.
b. To be a toll collector on a turnpike or thruway.
c. To be a wiper at the local car wash.

Sometimes the family begins to brainstorm new ideas for a Rank Order which grows out of ranking experiences like the one above. This example came in that way:

Which of these three things that might happen at Thanksgiving would bother you the most?

a. Having to work in the pickle factory all day on Thanksgiving.
b. If mother didn't cook and we sent out for a pizza for Thanksgiving dinner.

c. If she did cook the works, complete with pumpkin pie, chestnut stuffing, etc., and the family ate it in twelve and one-half minutes and then all rushed in to watch a football game and left her with the gravy slowly congealing on the plates.

Once a family gets the hang of Rank Orders, it can make them up about all kinds of issues: current events, family conflicts, hopes and goals, and priorities the family needs to establish about many things.

Twenty Things You Love to Do

Some evening, after the main course and before dessert, give each member a piece of paper and a pencil and ask each of them to number from 1 through 20 down the center of the piece of paper.

Ask each member to list twenty things, any twenty things, he or she loves to do in life. They can be as small as going for the mail or as big as celebrating Christmas. The only criterion is that the person writing really loves doing it. Try to be silent while people are thinking. Give them lots of time to compile their list.

When everyone has completed his list, the lists need to be coded by each individual. Here are some possible codings. Each family can think of others.

1. Put a dollar sign by each item that requires an outlay of at least three dollars any time you do it.
2. Place a P by each item which is more fun for you to do with people and an A by each item which is more pleasurable for you to do alone.
3. Put a 5 in front of any item which would not have been on a similar list if you had done one five years ago.
4. Use the letters PL for any item which requires planning.
5. Put a D in front of anything you love to do which probably would be disapproved of by most of the neighbors.
6. Finally, for each item on your list of twenty, record the date when you did it last.

After the codings are finished, ask members of the family to make what we call I Learned Statements. They are simply sentences which go: "I learned that I . . ." or "I noticed that I . . ." or "I relearned that I. . . ."

One thing about the Twenty Things You Love to Do exercise is that it can be done more than once. In fact, the more a family begins to examine what it does, alone and together, the more life changes and the more those things we place on a list of items we love to do change, too. That is the way it is with values. They are not locked in cement for life. New data make new values. And clarifying those values generates a deeper awareness. One of the real outcomes is that more of us refuse to settle for less than we want from life. We don't kill time with aimless TV watching. We try to live what we love. Knowing what we love is the first step.

Simple "Starters" for Following the Blessing

How nice it would be if there were more beautiful words following the blessing than "pass the butter." Some families include each member in sharing a small part of his life *before* the food gets passed. For example, each member could share the high point of his day. The person who can't think of a high point has something to talk about, too: "What kind of day is it when you don't have a high point?"

Another starter could be based on: "Were you in sharp disagreement with anyone today?" or "Who bestowed the most kindness upon you today?" or "What I Learned Statements could you make today?" or "When did you like yourself the most today?" or "How could the day have been better?"

A few other ideas could start the evening meal. Have each person send an I Urge Telegram. Some evenings the telegram could be to a national or an international figure. Other nights it could be sent to someone at school or at work. A third option is to send them to members of the family. The telegram is simply a form for saying to each other important things that need to be said. If the tone of the meal gets established so children realize that this is a significant time, they will not gag or joke about the telegrams they send. They'll do it with deep feeling.

A tender way of getting each member of the family to share something is to do three rounds of I Wonder Statements. They are simple open-ended answers to the phrases: "I wonder why . . ." or "I wonder how come . . ." or "I wonder what would happen if . . ." or "I wonder why I. . . ."

What better time to keep alive the wonder in children than at the dinner table, right after the blessing and before the food is eaten?

Using a Value Sheet for a Longer Discussion

One of the most important strategies for clarifying values is a technique called the Value Sheet. People are asked to respond, usually in writing, to a highly charged, controversial statement. The writing is important. The discipline of putting thoughts on paper helps to clarify values. Value Sheets usually require you to write answers to four or five questions. All the questions are "you-centered." That is, they are questions which ask *you* to face up to where *you* stand on an issue. Finding out where *you* stand is one of the major objectives of value clarification. Read the article to everyone at the dinner table and get him to write out his answers to the five "you-centered" questions after the story.

We're Really Getting It Together, Man

"It's all a hassle, Man. The Establishment is forever trying to jive you. Well, I'm through with being jived, with being hassled. I'm just going to stay here on this mountain, smoke a lot of dope, and really get myself together."

It's been five years since you've seen them. And now somehow you hear they've moved West and are close by. There is more to it than old friend-ship. More like kin they were.

*   *   *

When Tommy comes through the door, he nods at you and goes right on by. It had been a while. He didn't recognize you. So you follow him, looking hard at him when he turns around. It finally dawns on him who you are. "How are you, Man?" he smiles.

Then, without another word, he sits down at the console, pulls out a pack-age of grass, and starts rolling joints. You look at him. He's wasted, gaunt; his eyes are kind of glazed-over remnants of faded blue. You finally get up to walk on. He is too spaced out.

He looks up, says, "You leaving? Come on back later and we'll rap." You say OK, but you have this feeling that you won't be doing that. Instead, you drive to where he and Laura live. Has she changed that much?

When you get there, you find out she has. You really don't believe what you see. Where once before was this beautiful, exciting woman there's now a drab little sparrow, living in a house without heat or water or electricity. Her clothes are rags. Her face is drawn and tight. Her eyes scare you.

*   *   *

But at least she's really happy to see you. And wants to talk: "Did Tommy do that?" she said, when you tell her of the scene at the station. "Wow, well, he's probably on cocaine. He stays stoked up all the time.

"I mean it's really beautiful for him, though. He glides through it all really well. He really works when he's stoned on drugs no matter how heavy they are. I can't handle it as much as he does. Like we both drop a lot of acid, but it's gotten where I don't need to but maybe every six weeks."

You hear her but you don't believe her. And you look at the filth and poverty and you ask her why. "Yeah, we're down to the wire, all right. But that's just for now.

"We're really getting it together, Man. I'm working with this great band and we're going to move to the city and Tommy's getting a job with this far-out station and . . ."

*   *   *

You listen. You're hearing the same thing you had talked about five years before. The same dreams. Laura keeps talking, but it starts making less and less sense. She uses the teenybopper terms "funky" and "out of sight" over and over.

It's a gray day with snow clouds hanging low over this secluded mountain town. The flakes finally start falling as you go back to pick up Becky.

"This is going to be a really far-out party," she tells you. The party. Right. You'd forgotten.

She tells you where to drive, up the mountain, on a dirt road that winds for eight miles. "Here's the place," she says, pointing to a wooden shack.

* * *

You go inside. Already there are ten people, young men and women, dressed in rags and tatters. They're already stoned. You walk in but nobody makes any move to introduce you. Becky lights up a joint, pours herself some wine, and sits down on a bed in the corner of the two-room house.

You sit and watch, waiting for some kind of conversation to begin. You look at Becky but she's spaced out, staring at the coal oil lamp as it provides a faded yellow parchment setting in the shack.

"Really far-out grass," a girl mumbles: "Yeah, really super grass," somebody else says.

You sit in the corner for three hours watching them "get it together." Looking at them "finding out where it's at." Five years is a long time. It really is.

Questions on "We're Really Getting It Together, Man":

1. List five immediate reactions you had to the story.
2. If the story is too anti-drug for you, tell why.
3. Tommy really seems to be fooling himself. How do you fool yourself sometimes?
4. Whom do you feel most sorry for in this story? Can you explain why you feel that way?
5. This is the hardest question for some people: What, if any, are the implications for your own life to be found in this Value Sheet exercise?

That is a Value Sheet. Any member can bring in the statement or story part of a Value Sheet. Then the family can rotate the responsibility for making up the questions to clarify the values. Any subject matter will do. All it need be is exciting, controversial, and full of values choices for the members of the family.

The Here and Now Wheel

A final game for the dinner table. I learned it from my colleague, Gerald Weinstein, at the University of Massachusetts. Each member draws a wheel and puts four spokes on it. On each spoke, each member lists exactly what he is now experiencing or feeling. It might be hunger or tiredness or anger or impatience or peacefulness. Each family member then writes two sentences about one of the spokes, one of the feelings. Expanding the feeling makes it more specific and more dimensional. These are shared around the dinner table. When family members get skillful at Here and Now Wheels, they are given the privilege of calling for anyone's Here and Now Wheel whenever a conflict develops or when one member in the family senses another member is going through something emotional which needs to be articulated.

I have shared a half dozen small ways of making the family dinner table a learning center. I have focused on the skills of values clarification, since I believe that they are among the most important heritages parents can leave with their children.

I would suggest a few cautions if you are drawn to these ideas for clarifying values and want to try them out on your own families. Don't use these exercises to ram home a predetermined outcome. Don't moralize unnecessarily or your children will turn you off like a record player with its needle stuck in a groove. All of these exercises must be kept open-ended. Your own sense of wonder, discovery, and amazement should be kept alive. Values clarification is the name of the process, not value inculcation. With the incredible future ahead of us all, we must affirm the idea that few of us can really know what our children should value. We can't tell them what to value. We can't be there all the time to value for them.

On the other hand, we as parents should make the clearest statements we can about where we stand. We should do it not punitively, not with flattery, not with manipulation. We need to be open and less uptight as we come in touch with alternatives for our family values which may be more creative than the ones we picked up during our own upbringing.

Finally, we must give dignity to the family's search for its meaning. It is only as we teach a process, a way of negotiating the as yet unfathomable future, that we leave our children with an estate more valuable than stocks, bonds, jewels, or gold. We leave a way of making sense out of the confusion and conflict surrounding all of us. That way is called values clarification. There is an old Spanish proverb that goes, "The journey is more important than the inn." Take your own family on such a journey. And use the dinner table for the center of learning it is or can be.

HOW SIXTY TEACHERS LEARNED ———————
TO THINK LIKE CHILDREN ONCE AGAIN[5]

The authors were recently asked to design an evening program to help teachers relearn what is relevant and of value to elementary school children. We felt that if teachers could again experience some of the realities of a child's world, it would help them become more understanding and sensitive to the needs of children in their classrooms. Many years separated some of the teachers in the group from their own childhood and they had consequently forgotten much of what it meant to be a child. We felt it was important to refresh their memories and help them recall again some of the incidents of their own childhood because "back there," for all of us, personality was being shaped and formed for the person who was to later emerge as an adult.

We began, as we always do, with "Love and Care," a moment or two set aside for getting in touch with how we feel. We asked each teacher to close his or her eyes and go deep into their bodies to discover silent feelings there. This excursion into inner space had the group examine muscles, lungs, heart, and head for an awareness of what was going on at the moment. There was a time for allowing any thoughts to bubble to the surface of the mind for consideration. Then they were asked to give their first names and define a feeling of which they were aware . . . "happy, sad, tired, relaxed, excited, tense, hurried" were some of the responses. When asked if there was any way to care for these individual needs, one person asked for an aspirin and several asked for help to overcome the "tiredness" they felt. (All of them had taught school that day.)

A circle to deal with tired muscles was formed with each person placing his or her hands on the shoulders of the one to their right. Before we could even give instructions several people began to gently massage the neck and shoulders of the person next to them. This continued for some time amid the ah's, oh's, mmmmmmmmmmmmm's, and sighs as each person felt some of the tight tension dissolve into relaxation.

We asked that there be no talking, only sighing so that the quieting effect would be heightened. During this period we turned on a record player to soft, slow music. At a signal the group turned completely around and massaged the person who had been massaging them . . . a way to return in kind, an expression of gratitude.

Another ten to fifteen minutes was given to gently massaging the

[5]By Sidney B. Simon and Robert O'Rourke, from the January 1976 edition of the Newsletter of the Association for Humanistic Psychology.

forehead, temples and facial muscles. Half the group was seated and received the caring of the person standing behind them. Gently pressing the head, neck, and shoulders and then releasing was enjoyed by everyone. Backscratching prompted more sensuous groans of satisfaction and then the group exchanged places and those who had been standing received the whole repertoire of touch-caring as they had previously given it. Within twenty minutes the group felt alive and receptive, ready to experience what was to come next. (One teacher with a headache reported it had vanished—another spontaneously remarked, "I think my kids would really enjoy this experience.")

We then asked the teachers to mill around the room, nonverbally, and choose one other person to talk with. They were asked to close their eyes and remember back to their sixth grade room, to again go back to their room, with the desks, their classmates, the teacher, pictures on the wall, the smell of the place, etc. After a few moments they were asked to talk for three minutes about that nine-month period in their life. Their partner was to listen without interruption . . . three delicious minutes of uninterrupted talking, a rare experience for most people. We signaled for them to stop after three minutes and instructed the listener to report back what his partner seemed to value about school as a child. The process was then reversed while the other person talked without interruption to a person who really listened. Values were again discussed.

A second group of two was formed after again milling quietly. The newly formed pair was asked to close their eyes and go back to an earlier period of childhood, age eight or nine, and recall from the past one thing they hear their mother saying to them . . . and after that what they hear their father saying. This is in turn discussed without interruption for three minutes each, with the listener asking the question, "What impact did these 'sayings' have on you then and to what extent has it influenced the way you are now?"

Back in the large group we asked each teacher to make a nametag with the following information written on it:

1. One highlight of last week in teaching.
2. Two people in your school who nourish you.
3. Two things that restored your faith in education last week.
4. Your most successful year in the teaching profession.
5. One thing you look forward to next week.
6. One thing you dislike about children and what you do about that.

Again the teachers milled nonverbally choosing a partner and then choosing another group of partners to form a group of four. The group then decided which person would talk for four minutes, which one for three minutes, two minutes, and one minute. As before the talking was to be uninterrupted. The first subject was:

Remember one pleasant thing that happened to you before you went to school in the first grade. Each teacher in turn talked about this childhood incident for his or her alloted time. (This strategy elicits memories of happiness, things of value, what is important to children.)

The second task was to recall a "Cookie Person" in their life, a person (man or woman) who nourished and loved them as a child. The teachers chose the length of time they needed for this discussion—four, three, two, or one minute. (Our "Cookie Person" taught us much about loving and giving and how to express feelings with children.)

The third assignment was to recall taking a bath with someone at the age of five. The same time procedure was used. (Taking a bath with someone gave us some of our first values regarding sexuality and certainly a lot of our values about cleanliness.) The evening program ended with the teachers writing several

I learned statements

I wonder statements

I wish statements

Some of the following responses reflect the discovery-learning of the teachers:

"I learned some new relaxing techniques to use with my class and how to relax myself."

"I learned to set aside a time for loving and caring for my children."

"I learned to be a better listener."

"I learned to express more what I feel."

"I learned some neat ways to get to know people. There are sure some super people around."

"I learned to understand myself better and I learned everyone needs recognition."

"I wonder if I hide myself too much from kids."

"I wonder what would happen if I touched and validated my children more."

"I wonder if there will ever be enough 'soft and warm' to go around."

"I wonder about all the others I didn't have a chance to meet tonight."

"I wonder what would happen if we were more considerate of children's feelings and less about academics and order."

"I wish I could touch and hug everyone I wanted to."

"I wish I would take more time for these kinds of things for myself and my class."

"I wish we all could do this again sometime and I wish all the teachers in my building could do this just once together."

"I wish my class thought of me as their 'Cookie Person.' "

Two teachers approached us as the crowd began to disappear into the night, "We *wish* you would write an article about this evening's program and submit it for publication. We *wonder* what would happen if all or even parts of it were used in faculty meetings. We bet it would cause teachers to write hundreds of I *learned* statements that would benefit so many children." We responded with this short article and now *we wonder*.

"GETTING TO KNOW YOU"[6] ───────────────────

Teachers and others may accomplish much as they come to know one another's authenticity, realness, and aliveness. Four strategies for this purpose, and the steps by which they may be carried out, are suggested here.

When Anna was called to the small country of Siam to teach the King's household, her conviction was that it was essential "to get to know" the children at an intimate level before she taught them. "Getting to know all about them" was Anna's way of caring, her way of prizing them as individuals. Conversely it may be equally important for children to know and understand their teacher, to reach out to the teacher in a more personal way.

It is intriguing to the authors as they work with groups how much people are interested in knowing them on more human terms—to experience the authenticity, the realness, the aliveness of the teacher. In reciprocal, open, honest dialogue, learning becomes full of possibilities both for the teacher and learner, in fact this dichotomy of teacher (separated from, unknown to) learner becomes teacher-learner in an atmosphere of trust. Thus self-disclosure offers reciprocal growth possibilities.

We believe this more intimate relationship is especially important with children as, for example, when a teacher opens his or her life to them in quiet dignity by saying, "These are some of the things I believe in but I don't expect you to slavishly follow me or adopt my beliefs. I offer you my alternatives only for you to consider." In this thoughtful

---

[6]By Sidney B. Simon and Robert O'Rourke, published by Educational Leadership, Washington D.C., May, 1975.

way the teacher shows he or she too is searching for truth and is willing to share as a gift whatever wisdom he or she has discovered in the search.

To aid in this search for authenticity the authors offer four values clarification strategies as possible approaches to becoming real, honest human beings to students.

Strategy 1. "What I Believe"

Step 1: Write on a sheet of paper 15 things you love to do. In this way you inventory your life to discover what things make life most satisfying and meaningful.

Step 2: In order to help you clarify which of these "loves" are really important values that affect your behavior and thus are important for students to know ask yourself:

a. Have I chosen these loves freely?
b. Have I chosen them from among alternatives?
c. Are they chosen after some reflection and thought?
d. Do I prize and cherish them?
e. Do I publicly affirm them when appropriate?
f. Do I act upon them?
g. Are they part of a consistent pattern in my life?

Step 3: Choose any three of your loves that meet all seven of these demanding standards because these can be considered real values in your life. They have been established through your own experience; for now, at least, they provide your life with direction and purpose.

Step 4: Tom T. Hall, musician/composer, sings about the wisdom of an old black man he once met in Miami. The old man shared with him the idea that in all the world there were only three things that really added up as being important: "Old dogs, children, and watermelon wine"—a curious yet valid combination of loves from out of one man's experience (from the album, "Tom T. Hall . . . The Storyteller," Mercury Records). We now ask you to "boil down" your 15 loves to the 3 most important to you and then simply talk for a few minutes to your class about these priorities in your life. An interesting way to present this small segment of your life is to make a collage portraying these three loves. This can be accomplished through symbolism or actual photographs of the things, objects, and people whom you most love.

Step 5: After you have talked, invite your students to publicly interview you, thus providing them with further opportunity to know you more intimately.

Step 6:   Ask the group to write a series of sentences beginning with:

I learned _____.

I wish _____.

I was happy that _____.

I wonder _____.

I was surprised that _____.

Each student is asked to voluntarily give one or two statements from the above discoveries. Any student who does not wish to share his or her ideas has the option to pass at this time.

Step 7:   If your students seem interested in sharing their lives with you this 6-step strategy could then be used on successive days with each class member as focus person.

Strategy 2. "Life Inventory"[7]

This strategy helps both teacher and student look at the major themes and events of their lives:

    a. What are some of the happiest things I can remember?
    b. What do I do well?
    c. How have I shown courage in my life?
    d. What have been turning points in my life?

These and other questions can bring the teacher's life into focus and, in turn, can make students more visible to the teacher if they share their lives in this way.

Strategy 3. "Contract with Myself"

To clarify where you are now and what you strive for in life is an important consideration. Life, to be most zestful and alive, must have meaning and focus. This strategy can have a personal clarifying effect for your life as well as help students gain some idea of "where you are coming from."

Using words or pictures in a collage to visually portray your search, consider the following:

[7]From Sidney Simon *et al. Values Clarification, A Handbook of Practical Strategies for Teachers and Students.* Hart Publishing Co., New York, 1972.

Where I am now?

Barriers to becoming

What I want.

Strategy 4. *"My Personal Story"*

Sam Keen in his exciting book, *To a Dancing God*, suggests that each of us, sometime, should have an opportunity to write our own autobiography—our own story as a way to discover personal identity. He suggests several, central questions that help any individual discover a practical philosophy of life.[8]

"How did I come to be as I presently am?"

"What wounds or hurts do I resent having suffered?"

"Who were my important heroes and models?"

"What gifts was I given for which I am thankful?"

"What were critical decisions for which I was responsible?"

"If everything goes perfectly for me, how will things be in ten years?"

"What will I be doing? Feeling?"

"What things will I have?"

"What relationships?"

"What will I be looking forward to ten years from now?"

These questions underscore the idea that the *past* most certainly exists as a part of us now but in the same way the *future* also exists within us now. "That which the person *is* and that which the person *could be* exist simultaneously . . . thereby resolving the dichotomy between Being and Becoming."[9]

In summary, our thesis is that as a basis for effective learning the teacher must be known—the student also must be known—thus mutual needs are brought to awareness and then have a good chance to be reciprocally met. Sidney Jourard has posed two questions: "How can I love a person whom I do not know? How can the other person love me if he does not know me?"[10]

In these four strategies we have sought to reduce the mystery that

---

[8]Sam Kee,. *To a Dancing God.* Harper & Row, Publishers, New York, 1970, p. 73.
[9]Abraham Maslow, *Toward a Psychology of Being.* Van Nostrand Reinhold Company, New York, 1968, p. 160.
[10]Sidney Jourard, *Transparent Self.* Van Nostrand Reinhold Company, New York, 1964, p. 25.

sometimes exists between teacher/learner in hopes that an I/Thou relationship may be established which will, in turn, promote the reaching of
common education goals and objectives, each having mutual, personal
meaning.[11]

[11]If you want to receive a bibliography on Values Clarification Materials and a listing
of where workshops are being offered, send a self-addressed, stamped envelope to:
Dr. Sidney B. Simon, Box 846, Leverett, Massachusetts 01054.
Robert O'Rourke, 3809 Crescent Drive, Ft. Collins, Colorado 80521, also conducts
human growth workshops.